Judi Sunderland and Janet Inglis

ESSENTIALS

GCSE D&T
Food Technology

Contents

Contents

Eating for Health

Our Diet

It's important to choose a variety of foods to ensure that we obtain the range of nutrients, i.e. proteins, carbohydrates, fats, vitamins and minerals, which we need to stay healthy.

There are guidelines about the amount of nutrients needed by different people. These include **dietary reference values** (**DRV**), **estimated average requirements** (**EAR**) and **reference nutrient intake** (**RNI**).

The Eatwell Plate

The **eatwell plate** shows the types and proportions of the four main food groups that are needed for a healthy balanced diet.

Look at the eatwell plate to see how much of your food should come from each food group. For example, fruit and vegetables should make up about one third of the total food per day we eat. Five portions a day are recommended. A portion is one piece of fruit, e.g. apple, banana, or 80g (approx. three heaped tablespoons).

You don't need to get the balance right at every meal, but try to get it right over time, e.g. a whole day or week.

Foods and drinks high in fat and/or sugar, aren't essential to a healthy diet, and shouldn't be eaten often.

The eatwell plate is suitable for most people, except…
- children under the age of two
- people under medical supervision
- people with special dietary needs.

People under medical supervision or with special dietary needs may wish to check with their GP or a registered dietician to be clear about whether the eatwell plate is suitable for them.

The eatwell plate

Use the eatwell plate to help you get the balance right. It shows how much of what you eat should come from each food group.

Fruit and vegetables

Bread, rice potatoes, pasta and other starchy foods

Meat, fish, eggs, beans and other non-dairy sources of protein

Foods and drinks high in fat and/or sugar

Milk and dairy foods

A Healthy Diet

A **healthy diet** shouldn't be boring. You should be able to achieve healthy eating by cutting down on fat (especially saturated fat), salt and sugars, and increasing fibre (non-starch polysaccharide or NSP).

To help consumers do this, many food manufacturers have voluntarily adopted a system of **traffic light labelling**:
- **Red** means the amount is high – eat occasionally.
- **Amber** means the amount is neither high nor low.
- **Green** means the amount is low – this is a good choice to make.

Some manufacturers use a different system based on **Guide Line Daily Amounts** (**GDA**). These labels show the percentage of sugar, salt, fat and calories in each **serving** of the product.

Traffic Light Labelling

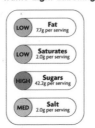

LOW — Fat 7.7g per serving
LOW — Saturates 2.0g per serving
HIGH — Sugars 42.2g per serving
MED — Salt 2.0g per serving

Guide Line Daily Amounts (GDA)

	Each 39g bar contains				
	Calories	Sugars	Fat	Saturates	Salt
	137	7.3g	3.3g	0.9g	0.1g
	7%	8%	5%	5%	2%

of an adult's guideline daily amount

Maintaining a Healthy Weight

By balancing the calories you eat with being physically active, you can maintain a **healthy weight**.

If you eat more calories than your body needs, it gets stored, as fat, and you'll become overweight. To reach a healthy weight you should follow a **calorie controlled diet**, which limits calorie intake, and have an active lifestyle.

If your weight increases to a point where it seriously endangers your health, you may eventually become **obese**.

Being overweight or obese increases the risk of developing…

- coronary heart disease (CHD)
- some cancers
- type 2 diabetes
- high blood pressure, which can lead to strokes
- osteoarthritis.

The **Food Standards Agency** (FSA) and the **Department of Health** (DH) are working together to tackle rising rates of **obesity**.

FOOD STANDARDS AGENCY

Being seriously underweight can also lead to health problems.

Healthy Weight, Healthy Lives

Many people in the UK are overweight or obese. **Healthy Weight, Healthy Lives** is a government strategy aimed at lowering obesity and excess weight.

The strategy…

- aims to support people to have a healthy diet combined with an active lifestyle
- aims to increase life expectancy
- should help to reduce the cost to the National Health Service (NHS) for the treatment of related health problems.

Quick Test

1. Which people should check with their GP whether the eatwell plate applies to them?
2. Obesity can increase the risk of developing coronary heart disease. **True** or **false**?
3. How can you maintain a healthy weight?
4. What foods should you cut down on to achieve a healthy diet?
5. Using the traffic light labelling system, a green light means that the food is a good choice to make. **True** or **false**?

KEY WORDS

Make sure you understand these words before moving on!

- Dietary reference values (DRV)
- Eatwell plate
- Healthy diet
- Traffic light labelling
- Guide Line Daily Amounts
- Healthy weight
- Obesity
- Healthy Weight, Healthy Lives

Eating for Health

Healthy Options

Manufacturers recognise that many consumers are concerned about healthy eating. They produce **healthy option foods**, because they know people will buy them, and it will increase their profit.

These foods make claims about…
- low fat
- low salt
- low sugar
- high NSP content.

It's important that consumers are able to understand what these claims mean, so they can make **informed choices** about buying food.

Nutrient	Definition	Content per 100g
Salt	Low salt High salt	Less than 0.3g 1.5g or more
Fat	Low fat High fat	Less than 3g More than 20g
Saturated fat	Low saturated fat High saturated fat	Less than 1.5g More than 1.5g
Sugar	Low sugar High sugar	Less than 5g More than 15g

Nutrient	Effect of Excess
Salt	High blood pressure Coronary heart disease
Fat	Overweight Obesity
Saturated fat	Raised cholesterol CHD
Sugar	Overweight Obesity Dental decay (caries)

Fortification

Fortification is the addition of **nutrients** to food.

Some foods must contain minimum amounts of nutrients by law, e.g. bread must have minimum amounts of calcium, iron and B vitamins, and margarine must contain Vitamins A and D.

Other foods are fortified voluntarily, e.g. breakfast cereals. This is used as a selling point, e.g. in food for children and babies.

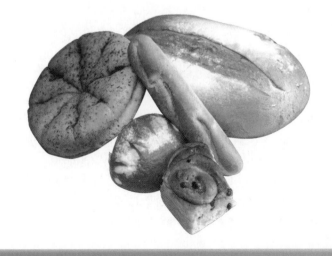

Nutritional Profiles

Nutritional profiles show the amount of each nutrient in a dish and the energy in calories. Protein, fat and carbohydrates are **macro nutrients**. Vitamins and minerals are **micro nutrients**.

It's easy to compare the nutritional profile of dishes by looking at the nutrients per 100g of the product. A nutritional profile for any dish can be made by using a **nutritional analysis program** on a computer.

g	FOOD	Protein (g)	Fat (g)	CHO (g)	Sugar (g)	Starch (g)	Fibre (g)	kCal	KJ	Na (mg)	Ca (mg)	Fe (mg)	VitA (µg)	VitD (µg)	VitC (mg)	VitE (mg)
175	Lasagne (boil)	5.3	1.1	39	1	38	2.5	175	742	2	11	1	0.0	0.0	0.0	0.0
375	Whole Milk	12	15	18	18	0.0	0.0	248	1031	206	431	0.0	274	0.0	4	0.0
25	Margarine	0.0	20	0.0	0.0	0.0	0.0	185	760	200	1	0.0	383	2	0.0	2.0
25	Plain White Flour	2.5	0.3	20	0.0	20	0.9	88	373	1	38	1	0.0	0.0	0.0	0.0
2	Mustard Powder	1	1	0.0	0.0	0.0	0.0	9	38	0.0	7	0.2	0.0	0.0	0.0	0.0
100	Cheddar Cheese	26	34	0.0	0.0	0.0	0.0	412	1708	670	720	0.0	550	0.0	0	0.5
200	Raw Beef Mince	37.6	32.4	0.0	0.0	0.0	0.0	442	1824	172	30.0	5	0.0	0.0	0	0.2
400	Canned Tomatoes	4.0	0.4	12.0	11	1	3.2	64	276	156	48.0	2	880	0.0	48	4.9
100	Tomato Puree	5	0.0	13	13	0.3	2.8	68	357	240	48	1.6	1300	0.0	38.0	5.4
2	Oregano	0.0	0.0	1	0.0	0.0	0.0	6	26	0.0	32	0.9	83	0.0	0.0	0.0
		g	g	g	g	g	g			mg	mg	mg	µg	µg	mg	mg
1404	Totals	92	105	103	43	58	9	1696	7135	1647	1364	11	3469	2.2	90	13.0
1404	1	92	105	103	43	58	9	1696	7135	1647	1364	11	3469	2.2	89.8	13.0
100		7	7	7	3	4	1	121	508	117	97	1	247	0.2	6.4	0.9

Calories

The **energy** in food is measured in **kilocalories** or **calories**. Energy is used for all bodily functions, such as breathing, pumping blood, digestion and brain activity.

Your body uses energy even when it's asleep. The more active you are, the more energy you will need to take in from your food.

Activity	Approximate Calories Used in One Hour
Running	510
Walking	240
Watching football	120
Sitting at a computer	75

Quick Test

1. Why do manufacturers produce healthy option foods?
2. What is margarine fortified with?
3. A nutritional profile can be made using a computer. **True** or **false**?
4. Your body doesn't need energy when it's asleep. **True** or **false**?
5. Why does your body need energy?

KEY WORDS
Make sure you understand these words before moving on!
- Healthy option foods
- Fortification
- Nutritional profiles
- Calories

Proteins

Function of Protein

Protein is required in the body for **growth and repair**. Excess protein is used for energy or stored as fat.

Proteins in the Body

During digestion, proteins are broken up into **amino acids**. These are absorbed into the bloodstream and made into new proteins in the body.

Twenty different amino acids are found in plant and animal protein. Thousands of amino acids may be joined together to make one type of protein. The body can make eleven of the amino acids from other amino acids. The remaining nine amino acids have to be obtained from protein in the diet. These are known as the **essential amino acids**.

Sources of Protein

Essential amino acids are found in protein from animal tissue and from soya bean and quinoa. These foods have **High Biological Value** (HBV).

Protein from plant sources, other than soya bean and quinoa, has **Low Biological Value** (LBV). This is because it lacks one or more of the essential amino acids.

You should eat a variety of these foods together to ensure that your body receives all the essential amino acids, e.g. beans on toast, mixed bean salad.

Sources of High Biological Value protein are…
- milk and milk-based products, e.g. cheese, yoghurt
- eggs
- meat
- shellfish
- fish (eat 3 portions per week)
- soya bean and soya-based products, e.g. tofu
- quinoa.

Sources of Low Biological Value protein are…
- Quorn™ (mycoprotein)
- nuts
- pulses, e.g. peas, beans and lentils
- rice
- cereals (oats, wheat) and cereal-based products
- peanuts.

Animal Proteins

Plant Proteins

Plant-based Proteins

Plant-based proteins…
- are cheaper and quicker to produce than meat
- use less land for production than meat for one person
- can be stored very easily.

Examples of plant-based proteins are Quorn, TVP, tivall, tofu and bean curd.

Quorn™ is a mycoprotein, which is related to the mushroom.

TVP (textured vegetable protein) is made from soya beans.

Tivall…
- is made from wheat and vegetable protein
- has a similar texture to meat.

Tofu and **bean curd** are made from soya beans.

Properties of Plant-based Proteins

Plant-based proteins…
- are versatile – they can be bought in different forms, e.g. minced, chunks, fillets, etc.
- are bland so they can be flavoured easily
- are fortified with vitamins and minerals
- are colourless, so colour can be added easily during manufacture
- are easy to store
- are cheaper than meat or fish
- can be cooked in many different ways.

Who Eats Plant-based Proteins?

People eat plant-based proteins because they…
- don't want to eat food from an animal source due to **moral, religious** or **ethical beliefs**
- are conscious of '**healthy' eating**
- want to eat a **more varied diet**.

Soya is present in 60 per cent of processed foods.

Quick Test

1. Why is protein needed by the body?
2. What happens if we eat too much protein?
3. Tofu, tivall, tofu and bean curd are all plant-based proteins. **True** or **false**?
4. Plant-based protein foods are quicker and cheaper to produce than meat. **True** or **false**?
5. What are plant-based proteins fortified with?

KEY WORDS
Make sure you understand these words before moving on!
- Essential amino acids
- High Biological value
- Low Biological value
- Plant-based proteins
- Quorn™
- TVP
- Tivall

Fats

Functions of Fat in the Body

Fat **provides energy, keeps us warm, protects internal organs** (e.g. the kidneys) and **contains fat soluble vitamins A and D**.

The word 'fat' is used to describe fats and oils.

At room temperature fats are **solid** and oils are **liquid**. They come from plant and animal sources.

Animal Fats and Vegetable Fats (Oils)

Animal fats are found in...	Vegetable fats are found in...
• cream • dripping • lard • butter • suet • meat • oily fish (tuna, salmon, mackerel) • eggs • cheese • meat.	• seeds (rape, sunflower) • olives • soya beans • nuts (walnut, brazil, hazelnut), peanuts.

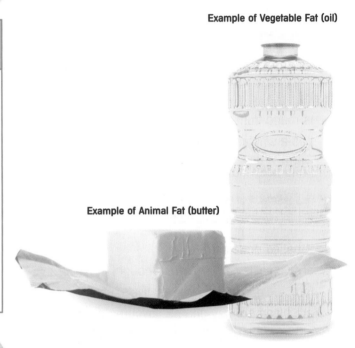

Example of Vegetable Fat (oil)

Example of Animal Fat (butter)

Types of Fat

Saturated fats raise the **cholesterol** level. This can lead to **health problems**, so foods containing saturated fats should be eaten sparingly, or replaced with healthier options. Examples of foods containing saturated fats are…

* meat pies
* sausages
* hard cheese
* coconut and palm oil
* butter
* ghee
* lard
* cream.

Hydrogen is bubbled through some oils to improve flavour and shelf life. This type of fat is known as **hydrogenated fat**. It's used by manufacturers to make margarine, spreads, pastry, cakes, biscuits and fast foods. Hydrogenated fat is as harmful as saturated fats.

Unsaturated (polyunsaturated) fats can help to reduce the level of cholesterol in the blood. Foods containing unsaturated fats include…

* oily fish
* avocados
* nuts
* seeds
* sunflower oil and corn oil
* walnut and rapeseed oil and spreads
* vegetable oils
* soya beans.

Functions of Carbohydrates

Carbohydrates have several uses in the body:
- They provide energy.
- NSP (**non-starch polysaccharide**), known as fibre, reduces the cholesterol in the blood.
- They help to eliminate waste products, as NSP cannot be digested.

Types of Carbohydrate

Carbohydrates are **sugars** and **starches**. Sugars are sweet and dissolve. Starches aren't sweet and don't dissolve. Sugars can be monosaccharides (simple sugars) or disaccharides (two sugars joined together).

Starches are known as **polysaccharides** (many sugars joined together).

The other type of carbohydrate is NSP.

Conversion of Carbohydrates

Sugars provide **instant energy**. Starches have to be digested into sugars before the energy can be released. So energy from starches is released more slowly.

Athletes, such as marathon runners or cyclists, eat starchy foods, e.g. pasta, before an event because they have a low glycaemic index (GI). This means that energy is released slowly through the race.

If you take in more carbohydrates than you need to use as energy, they are **stored as fat**. This can lead to you becoming overweight. It can eventually result in obesity and related health problems.

Sugar causes **tooth decay** and **dental caries**, so it's important to brush your teeth after eating sugary foods.

Quick Test

1. What are the functions of fat in the body?
2. Why is it better, as part of a healthy diet, to replace saturated fat with unsaturated fat?
3. Sugar is good for your teeth. **True** or **false**?
4. What is the correct word to describe a simple sugar?
5. Why do long distance runners eat starchy foods like pasta?

KEY WORDS

Make sure you understand these words before moving on!
- Animal fats
- Vegetable fats
- Saturated fats
- Cholesterol
- Hydrogenated fat
- Unsaturated fats
- Non-starch polysaccharide
- Monosaccharides
- Disaccharides

Vitamins

Vitamins are made up of…

- **carbon**
- **hydrogen**
- **oxygen**.

Many vitamins can't be stored or made by the body, so they need to be taken in each day. If you eat a wide variety of foods you should get all the vitamins you need, and you shouldn't need to take vitamin tablets or supplements.

Vitamins…

- prevent illness and maintain good health
- aid building and repair
- control the release of energy needed by the body.

Vitamins A and D are **fat soluble**. **Vitamins B and C** are **water soluble**.

Vitamin	Source	Function	Deficiency	Excess
A	Liver, egg yolk, margarine, dark leafy vegetables, red fruit and vegetables, e.g. carrots, mangos	Healthy eyes and bone growth	Vision problems, dry skin, slow growth in children	Orange tint to skin
D	Margarine, breakfast cereals, produced by the action of sunlight on skin	Strong teeth and bones	Rickets, osteoporosis, poor development of the unborn child	Can be poisonous
B Complex	Wholegrain cereals, yeast, meat	Releases energy from food	Beri beri	Not stored in the body
Folic Acid (B complex, folate)	Leafy green vegetables, pulses, bananas	Makes red blood cells	Neural tube defects, e.g. Spina Bifida in babies	N/A
C	Citrus fruits, green vegetables, blackcurrants	Helps iron absorption	Scurvy, slow healing of wounds	Water soluble, so lost in urine

Minerals and Water

Facts About Minerals

An adequate supply of **minerals** is essential for
good health. Minerals are used in building the body
and controlling how it works.

Mineral	Source	Function	Deficiency	Excess
Calcium (used with phosphorus)	Dairy products, green vegetables, bones in canned fish	Strong bones and teeth, blood clotting	Rickets, weak teeth, muscle and nerve problems	N/A
Phosphorus (used with calcium)	All plant and animal cells	Strong bones and teeth, energy release from food	N/A	Tetany, poor muscle tone
Sodium (salt)	Most fish, most manufactured food, monosodium glutamate	Water balance, nerve and muscle activity	Muscular cramps	Raised blood pressure, heart disease, stroke
Fluoride	Seafood, fluoridated water, some toothpaste	Protects teeth	Tooth decay	Brown spots on teeth
Iron	Meat, cocoa, dried fruit, green leafy vegetables	Transports oxygen in the body	Anaemia	Liver damage

Water

Water is essential for life. It's used to…
- control body temperature by perspiration
- lubricate joints
- maintain healthy skin
- prevent constipation.

Adults require 2–3 litres of water per day. Without
water the body becomes **dehydrated**, which can lead
to death. Excess water is normally excreted as urine,
but in some cases drinking too much may be fatal.

Quick Test

1. What is the chemical composition of vitamins?
2. Which vitamin is found in citrus fruits?
3. Vitamins A and D are water soluble. **True** or **false**?
4. An excess of which mineral increases the risk of heart disease and stroke?
5. A deficiency of which mineral can result in anaemia?
6. Excess water is stored in the body. **True** or **false**?

KEY WORDS

Make sure you understand these words before moving on!

- Vitamins
- Fat soluble
- Water soluble
- Minerals
- Calcium
- Phosphorus
- Sodium
- Fluoride
- Iron
- Water

Practice Questions

1. Which of the following statements are true? Tick the correct options.

    A   Five portions of fruit and vegetables should be eaten every day.   ◯

    B   Your body doesn't use energy when you're asleep.   ◯

    C   Vitamin tablets should be taken regularly.   ◯

    D   Food and drinks that are high in fat and sugar should be eaten daily.   ◯

    E   For a healthy diet you should cut down your NSP intake.   ◯

    F   The eatwell plate is suitable for teenagers.   ◯

    G   A nutritional profile lists the ingredients in a food.   ◯

    H   Being seriously underweight can lead to health problems.   ◯

2. What does DRV stand for?

    ....

3. Fill in the missing words to complete the following sentence.

    Manufacturers can make food healthier by .... the amount of

    ...., ... and ...., and by increasing the

    amount of ....

4. Circle the correct options in the following sentences.

    a) Obesity can cause **high blood pressure** / **low blood pressure**.

    b) Obesity can lead to **constipation** / **diabetes**.

    c) Obesity in the UK is **increasing** / **decreasing**.

    d) Obesity can cause **coronary heart disease** / **anorexia**.

    e) Obesity can cause **dry skin** / **osteoarthritis**.

    f) Obesity can cause **gastroenteritis** / **some cancers**.

5. What is the difference between High and Low Biological Value proteins?

    ....

    ....

    ....

6 Which of the following statements apply to High Biological Value proteins? Tick the correct options.

A High Biological Value proteins mostly come from animals. ◯

B High Biological Value proteins contain essential amino acids. ◯

C High Biological Value proteins are bland, so they can easily be flavoured. ◯

D High Biological Value proteins don't need a lot of land in their production. ◯

E High Biological Value proteins are found in 60 per cent of processed foods. ◯

F High Biological Value proteins are expensive to produce. ◯

G High Biological Value proteins are fortified with vitamins and minerals. ◯

H High Biological Value proteins are easy to store. ◯

7 Circle the correct options in the following sentences.

a) Plant-based proteins are **spicy** / **bland**.

b) Plant-based proteins are **easy** / **difficult** to store.

c) Plant-based proteins are present in **40 per cent** / **60 per cent** of processed foods.

8 Circle the correct options in the following sentences.

a) TVP is made from **broad beans** / **soya beans**.

b) Quorn™ is made from **mould** / **mycoprotein**.

c) Tivall is made from **vegetable and soya protein** / **wheat and vegetable protein**.

d) Tofu is made from **mushrooms** / **soya beans**.

9 Which of the following statements applies to carbohydrates? Tick the correct option.

A Carbohydrates contain all the essential amino acids. ◯

B Carbohydrates include sugars and starches. ◯

C Carbohydrates prevent constipation. ◯

D Carbohydrates are only found in animal sources. ◯

10 Which of the following statements applies to minerals? Tick the correct option.

A Minerals control body temperature. ◯

B Minerals come from animal and vegetable sources. ◯

C Minerals contain cholesterol. ◯

D Minerals can be made in the body. ◯

Medical Factors

Dietary Choices

The choices that people make about food depend on many factors, including…

- dietary and medical needs
- religion
- ethical reasons.

Food and Pregnancy   Edexcel • OCR

A pregnant woman needs the correct **balance of nutrients** so that she and her baby are healthy. She should avoid gaining more than 10–12 kilos in weight throughout the pregnancy and should eat…

- iron rich foods with foods containing Vitamin C
- foods containing calcium
- foods high in NSP
- foods high in **folic acid** to reduce the risk of Spina Bifida.

Food to Avoid During Pregnancy	Possible Problem	Effect
Raw or partially cooked egg	Salmonella	Food poisoning
Unpasteurised milk or milk products, e.g. Camembert, Brie, undercooked meat, cook-chill foods (unless heated thoroughly to 72°C), pâté	Listeria	Severe illness, miscarriage, still birth, baby with listeriosis – a serious illness
Liver and liver products	Excess Vitamin A	Too much can harm the baby
Undercooked meat (e.g. at BBQs), soil on fruit and vegetables	Toxoplasmosis	Miscarriage or still birth, blind baby
Shark, sword fish, marlin	Mercury	Harms development of the baby's nervous system

Coronary Heart Disease (CHD)   Edexcel • OCR

An **angina attack** happens when blood can't get to the heart to supply it with oxygen. This happens when the arteries leading to the heart have become narrower due to fatty deposits. A **heart attack** will result if the artery is completely blocked by a blood clot.

Factors which increase the risk of **coronary heart disease** are…

- high blood pressure
- smoking
- high cholesterol levels.

You can lower **cholesterol levels** by…

- reducing the amount of saturated fat in your diet
- increasing the amount of fruit and vegetables you eat
- taking regular exercise.

Diabetes

Diabetes is the third most common long-term disease in the UK. It can lead to complications such as…

- heart disease
- kidney disease
- blindness
- nerve problems, which may lead to limb amputations.

Diabetics can't produce sufficient **insulin** to control the **glucose** level in the blood.

There are two types of diabetes:

- **Type 1 diabetes**, which can be treated with insulin injections.

- **Type 2 diabetes**, also known as 'maturity onset', which can be treated with diet and exercise, but may require medication and / or insulin.

To prevent diabetes, you should eat a healthy, balanced diet and take regular exercise.

If you have diabetes, your diet should be…

- low in salt
- low in sugar
- low in fat
- high in fruit and vegetables
- high in starchy carbohydrates.

Diabetics don't have to cut out all sugar, but they should eat it in **moderation** as part of a healthy diet.

Lactose Intolerance   Edexcel • AQA

People can be intolerant of many foods.

Lactose intolerance is common; it affects about 70 per cent of the world's population, with wide geographic variations.

It can be temporary or permanent, and is caused by a lack of **lactase**, the digestive enzyme which breaks down the **lactose** (natural sugar) found in **cows**, **sheep** and **goats milk** into simple sugars.

If you suffer from lactose intolerance, you should avoid these types of milk and milk products, and replace them with alternatives such as **soya milk**.

Alpro Soya Milk

Quick Test

1. List three foods which pregnant women should avoid.
2. Why should sword fish be avoided during pregnancy?
3. List three things which can lead to CHD.
4. Diabetics can't eat any sugar. **True** or **false**?
5. Which enzyme is missing in people with lactose intolerance?

KEY WORDS

Make sure you understand these words before moving on!

- Folic acid
- Coronary heart disease
- Diabetes
- Lactose intolerance
- Lactase

Food Allergies and Intolerance

Allergies

All allergies involve the **immune system**, and are usually more serious than food **intolerance**.

Symptoms of allergies are…
- coughing
- dry throat
- nausea
- feeling bloated
- vomiting
- wheezing
- running or blocked nose
- sore red / itchy eyes.

Nut Allergies

In some people with a **nut allergy**, a very small amount (trace) is all that's needed to trigger anaphylaxis. **Anaphylaxis** is a severe allergic reaction, which causes swelling of the airways and lowering of the blood pressure. This may result in death unless it's treated quickly with an injection of adrenaline.

Food labels must state if a food contains nuts. It's also vital for manufacturers to include 'may contain nuts' on their product labels. This warns consumers that a very small amount of nut may have accidentally been in contact with their product, e.g. when food is processed where nut products have been made previously.

Coeliac Disease   Edexcel • AQA

Coeliac disease is an intolerance to gluten. **Gluten** is a protein found in wheat, barley and rye. Oats contain a similar protein and may also need to be avoided by coeliacs.

Coeliacs can't absorb nutrients if they eat gluten. This causes **malnutrition** and **anaemia**. Symptoms include diarrhoea and weight loss.

Coeliac disease can also cause bone disease, certain cancers and growth problems in children. There is no cure for coeliac disease, but it's treated by not eating foods that contain gluten.

Corn, rice and potatoes don't contain gluten. You can also buy special gluten-free products, e.g. bread and biscuits.

Products displaying the Crossed Grain symbol have been licensed by Coeliac UK and are safe to eat for those following a gluten-free diet.

Religion

Followers of some religions are required to follow certain dietary rules.

'**Kosher**' or '**halal**' meat is slaughtered in a special way.

Religion	Dietary Requirement(s)
Judaism	No shellfish or pork. Only 'kosher' meat. No dairy products and meat in the same meal.
Hinduism	No beef or beef products.
Sikhism	No beef. May be vegetarian.
Islam	No pork. Only 'halal' meat.

Ethical Issues

People avoid eating **meat** because of their religious beliefs, concern about the **environment**, and associated health risks.

In the 1990s, concerns over **bovine spongiform encephalopathy** (**BSE**) and its links with the fatal human equivalent, **Creutzfeldt-Jakob's Disease** (**CJD**), contributed to a decline in the demand for beef products. **Bird flu** has had a similar effect on the sales of chicken and turkey.

The amount of **fish** being eaten in the UK is **increasing**, so there's a danger of fish supplies **running out**.

In order to avoid fish stocks running out…
* the way in which fish are caught is regulated
* fishing boats are restricted to a certain number of days at sea each year
* fish farms have expanded.

The **prawn fishing industry** is very energy expensive and wasteful. Prawns are caught by trawlers, which produce **greenhouse gases** (GHG), and are then transported across the world to be hand peeled, deep frozen and shipped back.

Quick Test

1. People with nut allergies can eat foods with nuts or traces of nuts in. **True** or **false**?
2. Coeliac disease is an intolerance to what?
3. Complete the following sentence: People who follow the Hindu religion don't eat

   _____ or

   _____ _____ .
4. To prevent fish stocks running out, fishing boats can only go to sea for a certain number of days each year. **True** or **false**?

KEY WORDS
Make sure you understand these words before moving on!
* Intolerance
* Nut allergy
* Anaphylaxis
* Gluten
* Malnutrition
* Anaemia
* Kosher
* Halal
* Environment
* BSE
* CJD
* Greenhouse gases

Ethics

Vegetarians and Vegans

Vegetarians don't eat meat, poultry, fish, or products such as gelatine, which are obtained by killing animals. Vegetarians do eat cereals, pulses, nuts, seeds, fruit and vegetables.

Lacto-ovo vegetarians eat eggs and dairy products, e.g. milk and cheese (made using vegetable rennet). Lacto vegetarians eat dairy products but not eggs and ovo vegetarians eat eggs but not dairy products.

The **vegetarian symbol**, found on food labels, indicates that a food is suitable for vegetarians to eat. It may not be suitable for **vegans**.

People are vegetarian because of **religious**, **ethical** or **moral** beliefs, for health reasons, or because they are **allergic** to animal products.

Vegans don't eat any food from **animal origin**. This includes meat, fish, poultry, dairy products, eggs and honey. The **vegan sunflower trademark logo** is found on products that have been registered with the Vegan Society, and are therefore free from animal involvement, in accordance with the Vegan Society standards.

Organic Farming

AQA • OCR

Organic foods are produced without the use of chemical pesticides, fungicides or synthetic drugs. They don't include genetically modified (GM) crops.

The market for organic foods is expanding. They appeal to consumers concerned about health, moral and ethical issues.

Choosing organic is a **lifestyle** choice, as there's no conclusive scientific evidence to show that organic food is more nutritious.

The table shows the advantages and disadvantages of producing organic food.

Advantages

- Improves soil quality
- Increases wildlife
- Reduces energy consumption, leading to lower carbon dioxide (CO_2) emissions
- Doesn't use fertilisers that contribute to greenhouse gas emissions

Disadvantages

- Food may be transported long distances
- Can be expensive to produce as yields are lower, so more land is needed
- Can encourage deforestation, increasing CO_2 production

The Red Tractor

The **Red Tractor** logo can only be used on food that has been produced, processed and packed to Red Tractor standards. The flag next to the Red Tractor logo shows the **country of origin**. When the union flag is used, it guarantees the food has been farmed in the UK and has reached agreed standards for food hygiene and safety, equipment used in production, animal health, environmental issues and responsible use of pesticides.

These standards are checked by inspectors trained by **Assured Food Standards** (AFS). This is a not for profit organisation.

Any product with this logo can be traced from farm to pack. The logo is used on meat, poultry, cereals, sugar beet, fruit and vegetables.

Global Dimensions

Fair trade is an independent consumer label, which guarantees that the farmers and workers in **lesser economically developed** (LED) countries receive a fair price for their goods.

The food must be produced in an **environmentally responsible** way. Workers benefit from investment in education, healthcare, farming improvements in their local area, and better working conditions. The fair trade logo is found on foods such as tea, coffee, chocolate, wine and bananas. The foods are produced in Asia, Africa, Latin America and the Caribbean.

Genetically Modified (GM) Foods

Genetically modified foods have had their **DNA altered** to give them a specific characteristic. They're being used more, especially in imported foods, but it isn't always possible to identify them. GM plant foods are being used to **increase crop production** in a world where food is becoming scarce.

It's possible to develop GM crops that require **less water**, so they can grow in dry areas of the world, can be **disease** and **pest resistant**, a **better colour**, have a **higher protein content**, or **withstand cold conditions**. It's thought that such plants will become more important in feeding the world in the future.

Quick Test

1. How do vegetarians know that a packaged food is suitable for them to eat?
2. Fill in the missing words: Organic foods are produced _____ chemicals. Buying organic foods is a _____ choice.
3. What do fair trade products guarantee for farmers and workers?

KEY WORDS
Make sure you understand these words before moving on!
- Vegetarians
- Ethical
- Vegans
- Organic
- Lifestyle
- Red Tractor
- Assured Food Standards
- Fair trade
- Genetically modified

Environmental and Social Issues

Environmental Issues

Environmental problems are a local, national and global issue, and co-ordinated planning is needed to solve them.

Recycle (this means re-use)
- Recycling is 'green'.
- It makes use of paper, metal and bottle banks or collection services.
- However, cleaning during recycling uses chemicals that cause pollution.
- Recycling a product sometimes uses more energy than making it from new resources.

Refuse
- Refuse to buy products with excess packaging.

Repair
- Repair equipment rather than replace it, at home and in industry.

Rethink
- Manufacturers must rethink the amount and type of packaging they use.

Reduce amount of packaging
- This might not appeal to customers.
- It might affect the end product.

Use renewable resources
- Renewable resources can be 'renewed' within 50 years.
- They don't use Earth's limited resources.

Use biodegradable packaging
- It's less harmful to the environment as it rots naturally.

Reducing Food Miles

Food miles refer to the distance food travels from where it's produced to where it's eaten.

Transportation by lorry, boat and plane creates carbon dioxide (CO_2), which contributes to global warming.

You can reduce food miles in the following ways:
- Use food in **season**.
- Use local food markets.
- Choose from sources nearest to the UK, e.g. grapes from Spain rather than South Africa.

- Use local and **regional producers**. Remember that heavily fertilised crops grown in heated greenhouses in Britain may create three times more emissions than continental equivalents that are flown here.

Striking a balance is important. If we only eat local produce, people in poor countries will not be able to sell their crops and will suffer financial hardship.

Recycling and Producing Less Waste

The food we buy is usually packaged in some way. Manufacturing packaging materials uses energy.

Food manufacturers are being encouraged to use less packaging to help the environment.

You can help produce less rubbish by buying food with **minimal** or **recycled packaging**. Many products can be made from recycled packaging.

Recycling can save energy and so reduce greenhouse gas (GHG) emissions.

About one third of all food we buy isn't used. It may go out of date before we need it, or too much is prepared and the rest is thrown away. Waste is placed in **landfill sites** where it produces **methane gas**. This contributes to GHG emissions. Waste food can be composted at home.

Environmental and Social Issues

Avoiding Deforestation

Trees remove **carbon dioxide** (CO_2) from the atmosphere. If large forest areas are cut down to graze cattle or grow crops, CO_2 builds up. This contributes to **global warming**.

Palm oil is used by manufacturers in many products, like biscuits and cakes. Producing it has led to great areas of rain forest being cut down in parts of Asia. Many animals that live in the rain forests are in danger of becoming extinct.

Reducing Carbon Dioxide Emissions

The Earth is surrounded by CO_2 and other gases, which insulate it by stopping heat escaping.

As CO_2 emissions increase, the Earth traps more of the Sun's energy. This leads to **global warming** and damage to the ozone layer, which causes climatic changes.

These changes affect food and water supplies throughout the world.

The Sun and the Ozone Layer

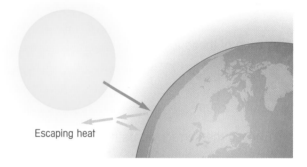

Escaping heat

Eating Less Beef and Lamb

Livestock, especially cows, produce **methane gas**, which is twenty times more harmful than CO_2. They produce more GHGs than the entire world's transport.

You could try eating more chicken and pork rather than beef and lamb.

Quick Test

1. What does the term 'food miles' mean?
2. Crops grown in heated greenhouses in Britain create less emissions than those flown in from Spain. **True** or **false**?
3. What type of gas is produced by food that's placed in landfill sites?
4. Which gas do trees remove from the air?
5. Which meats should we try to eat less of to help the environment?

Practice Questions

1 Circle the correct options in the following sentences.

a) Pregnant women should eat foods containing **mercury** / **calcium**.

b) Diabetics should eat sugar in **large amounts** / **moderation**.

c) People with lactose intolerance can't digest **milk** / **sugar**.

d) People with nut allergies can have a **severe** / **simple** reaction after eating nuts.

e) Coeliacs shouldn't eat gluten, which is found in **wheat** / **water**.

f) Hindus don't eat **pork** / **beef**.

2 What is the difference between vegetarians and vegans?

....

....

....

3 Which of these foods will a vegetarian eat? Tick the correct options.

A Apples ⬭   **B** Honey ⬭   **C** Pork ⬭

D Eggs ⬭   **E** Bread ⬭   **F** Beans ⬭

4 Choose the correct words from the options given to complete the following sentences.

environmentally	**farming**	**tea**	**fair price**	**education**
	Africa	**farmers**	**goods**	

Fair trade is an independent consumer label which guarantees that the .... and

workers in lesser economically developed (LED) countries in the world receive a

.... for their .... The food must be

produced in an .... responsible way. Workers also benefit from investment in

.... , healthcare, ... improvements in their local area, and

better working conditions. The fair trade logo is found on foods such as .... , coffee,

chocolate, wine and bananas, which are produced in Asia, ... , Latin America and

the Caribbean.

5 Which of the following statements are true? Tick the correct options.

    A   Products with a Red Tractor logo have a flag on them to show the country of origin. ⬭

    B   Any product with a Red Tractor logo has been checked by an Environmental Health officer. ⬭

    C   The Red Tractor logo is found only on milk and milk products. ⬭

    D   The Assured Food Standards Agency makes a lot of money by checking foods. ⬭

    E   The Red Tractor logo shows the consumer that the food has reached agreed standards for animal health. ⬭

6 Why are GM plant foods being used?

....

....

....

7 Choose the correct words from the options given to complete the following sentences.

thrown away   **methane**   **GHG**   **one third**   **landfill sites**   **out of date**

About .... of all food bought is not used. It may go

.... before it is used, or too

much is prepared and then .... This is then placed in

.... where it produces .... gas

contributing to ....

8 How would eating less beef and lamb help the environment?

....

....

9 Why is palm oil production damaging the environment?

....

....

....

Meat

Sources of Meat

Animals, **poultry** and **offal** are the three main sources of meat.

Mechanically recovered meat (MRM) is made by pressure blasting the animal carcass against a sieve after the prime cuts have been removed. This produces a slurry, or paste, which is used in products like sausages and economy burgers. It's much cheaper than normal cuts of meat.

Sources	Meat
Animals	Pork, beef, venison, lamb
Poultry	Turkey, duck, chicken, goose
Offal	Kidney, liver, tripe, tongue

Cooking Meat

Cooking meat makes it tender, makes it easier to digest, and kills bacteria.

When you heat meat...
- it changes colour
- connective tissue becomes gelatine
- extractions are released
- **non-enzymic browning** takes place.

The **high temperatures** used to fry meat before casseroling **seal** in the juices and **add colour**.

You should cook meat thoroughly until the juices run clear. Use a **probe** to check that the meat has reached the **correct temperature**.

The table shows the different methods of **tenderising** meat.

Method	How to Tenderise
Marinating	Use an acid, e.g. tomato, wine, yoghurt
Mechanical	Mince or flatten the meat with a mallet
Ageing	Hang the meat to allow natural enzymes to act
Using artificial substances	Add concentrated enzymes; these are sold as 'meat tenderisers'

Storing Meat

You should store meat and poultry...
- on the bottom shelf of the fridge to prevent liquid dripping onto other food
- in a clean, sealed container.

Keep cooked and raw meat separate to **avoid cross contamination**.

When **freezing** and **defrosting** meat, remember...
- to always freeze meat before its sell-by date
- that you can defrost meat in a microwave, but you should then cook it immediately
- to defrost meat in the fridge if you're not using it straight away
- that you can refreeze meat if it has been cooked
- to only reheat cooked meat once after it has been defrosted.

Types of Fish

There are three main types of fish:
- **oily fish**
- **white fish**
- shellfish.

Examples of **oily fish** are herring, mackerel, trout, salmon, tuna and sardines.

White fish can be round or flat.

Examples of **round fish** are cod, haddock, coley and whiting.

Examples of **flat fish** are plaice, turbot, halibut and sole.

Shellfish can be **crustaceans** or **molluscs**.

Examples of **crustaceans** are crabs, lobsters, prawns and shrimps.

Examples of **molluscs** are oysters, scallops, cockles and mussels.

Storing and Preparing Fish

Fish is a moist protein food. It is **high risk** because it is prone to carrying **bacteria**.

Fresh fish should be used as soon as possible or covered and stored in the fridge.

A lot of fish is prepared and **frozen at sea**, so it remains in peak condition until it is processed.

There are several ways to prepare fish:
- You can eat **hot smoked** fish, e.g. mackerel and salmon, without cooking it.
- You need to cook **cold smoked** fish, e.g. haddock, before you can eat it.
- Oily fish and shellfish, e.g. tuna, salmon and prawns, can be canned. They're stored in brine, tomato sauce or oil.
- Fish starts to coagulate (set) at 60°C. So when you are frying, grilling or baking fish, you need to enrobe it, i.e. give it a protective coating like flour, breadcrumbs or batter.
- You can steam or poach fish without a coating.

Quick Test

1. Meat comes from animals and birds. **True** or **false**?
2. Which acids can be used to marinate meat?
3. Name three fish that may be canned.
4. Fish must always be enrobed. **True** or **false**?

KEY WORDS

Make sure you understand these words before moving on!
- Poultry
- Offal
- Mechanically recovered meat
- Non-enzymic browning
- Tenderising
- Oily fish
- White fish
- Coagulate
- Enrobe

Milk

Milk

Milk…
- mostly comes from cows and has a layer of cream on top
- can be **homogenised** by forcing milk through tiny holes under great pressure, so the fat globules break down and can't reform
- deteriorates quickly, so it's heat treated to extend its shelf life and kill bacteria.

Primary Processing of Milk

Milk is processed in the following ways:
- **Pasteurised** whole milk is heated to 72°C for 15 seconds and cooled rapidly to 10°C or below.
- **Skimmed** milk is pasteurised with all the cream removed.
- **Semi-skimmed** milk is pasteurised with some of the cream removed.
- **Ultra heat-treated** (**UHT** or long life) milk is heated to 132–140°C for 1 second before being cooled rapidly.
- **Sterilised** milk is homogenised, bottled, sealed and heated to 110°C for 30 minutes, which alters its taste.
- **Dried milk** is less bulky to store and keeps without refrigeration. To produce it, water is evaporated, leaving a fine powder. It's the type of milk most often used by manufacturers.

There are two types of **canned milk**:
- In **evaporated milk**, water is evaporated off, making it more concentrated and sweeter. It's homogenised, sealed in cans and sterilised.
- **Condensed milk** is evaporated milk that isn't sterilised. Extra sugar is added, making it thick and sweet.

Different Types of Milk

Lactose Intolerance

Edexcel • AQA

People with **lactose intolerance** can substitute cows, sheep and goats milk in their diet with…
- soya milk
- rice milk
- coconut milk
- oat milk.

These types of milk don't contain lactose.

Alternative Milks

Secondary Processing of Milk

Secondary processing of milk produces other dairy products:

- **Butter** is made by churning cream. Types of butter are salted, unsalted, continental, clarified and ghee. Butter may be added to some margarines to improve their flavour.
- **Cream** is made from the fat in milk. Types of cream are single, whipping, double and extra thick. Cream can be **further processed** to make crème fraîche, clotted cream and soured cream. On heating, cream may separate.
- **Cheese** is milk in a solid form. It's approximately one third each of protein, fat and water. Many different cheeses are available, depending on the method of production used. When cheese is heated, the fat melts and separates; the protein coagulates and shrinks, making the cheese difficult to digest.
- **Yoghurt** is made by adding a bacterial culture to milk. Probiotic products, e.g. yoghurts and yoghurt drinks contain billions of live bacteria, which are beneficial to the digestive tract.

Storing Dairy Products

You should keep dairy products in the fridge, except for dried, condensed and evaporated milk.

Quick Test

1. Why is milk heat treated?
2. What temperature is used to pasteurise milk?
3. Which milk is most often used by food manufacturers?
4. Name four different dairy products.
5. How is yoghurt made?

KEY WORDS

Make sure you understand these words before moving on!

- Homogenised
- Pasteurised
- Skimmed
- Semi-skimmed
- Ultra heat-treated (UHT)
- Sterilised
- Dried milk
- Secondary processing

Cereals, Fruit and Vegetables

Cereals

Cereals...
- are the **edible seeds** of cultivated grasses
- are part of basic diets throughout the world
- contain a high proportion of **carbohydrate** in the form of starch
- are a valuable source of protein, **NSP** (fibre), vitamins and minerals.

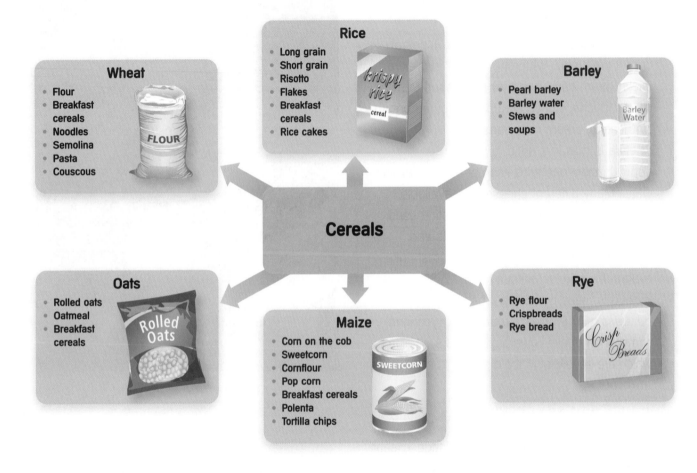

Wheat
- Flour
- Breakfast cereals
- Noodles
- Semolina
- Pasta
- Couscous

Rice
- Long grain
- Short grain
- Risotto
- Flakes
- Breakfast cereals
- Rice cakes

Barley
- Pearl barley
- Barley water
- Stews and soups

Cereals

Oats
- Rolled oats
- Oatmeal
- Breakfast cereals

Maize
- Corn on the cob
- Sweetcorn
- Cornflour
- Pop corn
- Breakfast cereals
- Polenta
- Tortilla chips

Rye
- Rye flour
- Crispbreads
- Rye bread

Fruit and Vegetables

Fruit and vegetables are available all year round, due to improved technology, production methods and better transportation links. Good quality fruit and vegetables can be **preserved** in the home by **freezing**, **pickling** and **jamming**.

Fruit and vegetables are used for their **organoleptic properties**:
- colour
- texture
- flavour
- smell.

You should prepare fruit and vegetables carefully to reduce nutrient loss:
- Prepare them just before use.
- Peel them thinly or use the skin.
- Don't chop them into small pieces.
- Don't store them in water.
- Cook them quickly in a small amount of liquid, using a lid, or steam or microwave them.
- Serve them quickly when they're cooked.
- Eat them raw if possible.

Classification and Size of Eggs

Class A eggs…
- are clean
- are fresh
- have unbroken shells.

Class B eggs are removed from their shells and pasteurised.

The size ranges from very large to small.

Size	Weight
Very large	More than 73g
Large	63–73g
Medium	53–62g
Small	53g

All eggs sold in Britain must be marked with a code that shows…
- which egg producer they come from
- the country of origin
- the type of production method used, e.g. free range, barn, etc.

Understanding Egg Codes

1UK12345

1 = F/Range
UK = Origin
12345
123SCO } Farm ID

Manufacturers use liquid, frozen or spray dried Class B eggs to reduce the risk of food poisoning.

You should **store** eggs…
- in the fridge with the blunt end upwards
- away from strong smelling foods.

Always use eggs by the best before date.

Functions of Eggs

Eggs have a variety of functions:
- **Coagulation** – egg white proteins coagulate (set) at 60°C, yolk proteins at 70°C for **thickening**, e.g. egg custard, lemon curd.
- **Aeration** – e.g. swiss rolls, meringues and mousses.
- **Emulsification** – egg yolks emulsify, e.g. mayonnaise.

- **Binding** – holds ingredients together, e.g. mincemeat in beefburgers.
- **Coating** – prevents food falling apart or absorbing too much fat, e.g. fish, chicken.
- **Glazing** – gives an attractive finish, e.g. pastry.
- **Garnish** – e.g. savoury dishes.
- **Enriching** – e.g. add to mashed potato to improve its nutritional value.

Quick Test

1. What are cereals?
2. What is the main carbohydrate found in cereals?
3. Why are fruit and vegetables available all year round?
4. Why should fruit and vegetables be cooked in a small amount of water?
5. Food manufacturers use fresh eggs in their products. **True** or **false**?
6. What happens to eggs when they're heated?

KEY WORDS

Make sure you understand these words before moving on!
- Edible seeds
- Carbohydrate
- NSP
- Class A
- Coagulation
- Aeration
- Emulsification
- Binding
- Coating
- Glazing
- Garnish
- Enriching

Fats and Oils

Sources of Fats and Oils

Fats and oils are produced from three different sources:

- **animal**, e.g. pigs, cows, sheep
- **vegetable**, e.g. wheat, barley, oats, seeds, olives, beans, some fruit (avocado)
- **fish**, e.g. trout, mackerel, salmon, herring.

Types of Fat

Fat is a solid at room temperature. **Oil** is liquid at room temperature.

You should store…

- fats in the fridge to avoid melting
- oils at room temperature, as they **solidify** in cold temperatures.

There is a demand for **low fat** or **reduced fat** products, because fat is high in calories. Some fat is needed by the body, but too much can cause you to become overweight or obese.

Types of oil:
- Olive oil
- Rape-seed oil
- Sesame seed oil
- Fish oils
- Sunflower oil

Types of fat:
- Soft margarine
- Hard margarine
- Dripping
- Lard
- Butter
- Low fat spread
- Suet

Functions of Fat

Fat has a variety of functions.

What it Does	Examples
Adds flavour	Butter in shortcake biscuits, cakes, breads, sauces, olive oil drizzled on pizza
Adds texture	Biscuits and pastries have a **short** (crumbly) texture, because the flour particles are coated in fat
Adds colour	Pastry and cakes
Aerates	Traps air when creamed with sugar in cake mixtures
Extends shelf life	Fat in baked products keeps them moist for longer

Sugar

Sugar cane and **sugar beet** are processed in order to produce many different kinds of sugar: caster, granulated, dark brown, soft brown, preserving sugar, muscovado, icing sugar, demerara, sugar cubes and molasses.

Eating too much sugar leads to the build up of plaque and tooth decay. **Plaque** is a sticky substance made up of bacteria, which is found on the teeth. The bacteria break down sugar and produce acid that destroys the enamel of teeth.

When a sugar solution is heated to a very high temperature it thickens and turns brown, adding flavour and colour. This is known as caramelisation. If the solution is overheated it blackens and produces an unpleasant taste.

Dextrinisation takes place when starch is cooked in a dry heat, e.g. an oven or grill. It's broken down into a simple sugar (dextrin).

Artificial sweeteners are low in calories. Manufacturers often use a mixture of artificial sweeteners.

Bulk sweeteners are similar in taste to sugar and are used in similar amounts in recipes. Examples are sorbitol, mannitol and xylitol.

Intense sweeteners are used in small amounts as they're much sweeter than sugar. Examples are saccharine, aspartame and acesulfame.

Functions of Sugar

What it Does	Examples
Sweetens	Cakes, biscuits, cooked fruit
Adds colour	Browning cakes by caramelisation and dextrinisation
Flavour enhancer	Tomatoes, baked beans, canned vegetables
Aerates	Traps air when creamed with fat
Decorates	Sprinkled sugar, butter icing, icing
Speeds up fermentation	Provides food for yeast

Quick Test

1. What is the difference between a fat and an oil?
2. The word 'short' means to have a crumbly texture. **True or false?**
3. How does the use of fat extend the shelf life of a product?
4. From which plants is sugar produced?
5. Why is sugar bad for your teeth?
6. Sugar is used in savoury products as well as sweet ones. **True or false?**

KEY WORDS
Make sure you understand these words before moving on!
- Fat
- Oil
- Solidify
- Low fat
- Reduced fat
- Short
- Tooth decay
- Plaque
- Caramelisation
- Dextrinisation

Practice Questions

1 Choose the correct words from the options given to complete the following sentences.

slurry   **meat**   **sausages**   **removed**   **sieve**   **pressure**   **blasting**

Mechanically recovered meat (MRM) is made by _____ _____ the

carcass against a _____ after the prime cuts have been _____.

This produces a _____, or paste, which is used in products like

_____ and economy burgers. It's much cheaper than normal cuts of _____.

2 Which of the following statements are correct? Tick the correct options.

    A Cooking meat makes it tough.

    B Cooking meat makes it easier to digest.

    C Pork should be cooked until the juices run clear.

    D Marinating meat makes it cook quicker.

    E When meat is cooked gelatinisation takes place.

    F Cooked meat can be reheated several times.

    G Cross contamination can take place if raw and cooked meat are stored together.

3 Circle the correct options in the following sentences.

    a) **Salmon** / **haddock** is an oily fish.

    b) **Sardine** / **cod** is a round white fish.

    c) **Plaice** / **tuna** is a flat white fish.

    d) **Prawns** / **oysters** are crustaceans.

    e) **Crabs** / **mussels** are molluscs.

4 Why is fish a high risk food?

_____

_____

5 Fill in the missing words to complete the following sentence.

_____ milk is made by forcing _____ through

_____ under great _____, so the fat

globules _____ down and _____ reform.

6 Draw lines between the boxes to match each type of milk with a statement that describes it.

UHT milk	The type of milk often used by manufacturers
Sterilised milk	Has some of the cream removed
Dried milk	Sealed in a can
Evaporated milk	Heated to 72°C for 15 seconds and cooled rapidly to 10°C or below
Pasteurised milk	Has its flavour altered
Semi-skimmed milk	Also known as 'long life' milk

7 What kind of milk doesn't contain lactose?

....

8 Circle the correct options in the following sentences.

a) Butter is made by **creaming** / **churning** milk.

b) Cream is made from the **fat** / **sugar** in milk.

c) Cheese is milk in a **liquid** / **solid** form.

d) Yoghurt is made by adding **bacteria** / **butter** to milk.

9 Choose the correct words from the options given to complete the spaces in the table.

lemon curd   **pastry**   **fish**   **mayonnaise**   **beefburgers**   **swiss roll**   **savoury dishes**

Function of Eggs	Example
Garnish	
Binding	
Glazing	
Emulsification	
Coating	
Aeration	
Coagulation	

Functional Properties of Food

Functional Properties of Food Edexcel • AQA

Food designers need to understand the properties of foods when they're designing new dishes, to make sure they match the **product profile**.

Solutions Edexcel • AQA

Examples of a **solution** are…
- fruit juice
- sugar and water syrups
- salt and water brine.

A solution is formed when…
- a liquid is dissolved in another liquid, for example fruit squash in water
- a solid is dissolved in a liquid, like sugar in a cup of tea.

Solutions (sols) will not separate when left to stand.

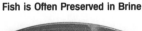

Fish is Often Preserved in Brine

Suspensions Edexcel • AQA

A **suspension** forms when solid particles are added to liquid but **don't dissolve**.

Starch particles, such as flour, don't dissolve in a liquid, but they form a **suspension**.

If the suspension isn't agitated (mixed), the solid particles fall to the bottom. One example is when a sauce mixture isn't stirred when heated and lumps form at the bottom of the pan.

Gels Edexcel • AQA

A **gel** is a solid, jelly-like substance. Gels are mostly liquid, but behave like solids due to the gelling agent holding the liquid in place. Gels form when starch is heated in a liquid and cooled (**gelatinisation**).

The table below shows examples of common gels.

Example of Gel	Gelling Agent
White sauce	Flour
Filling from a lemon meringue pie	Cornflour
Jam	Pectin
Flan glaze	Gelatine

Functional Properties of Food

Smart Starches
Edexcel • AQA

Manufacturers use a large number of starches, which have been altered to change their working properties. These are known as **modified starches** or **smart starches**:

- Some modified starches are pre-gelatinised. This allows them to thicken instantly, e.g. packet custard, pot noodles.
- Some modified starches allow sauces to be reheated with no **synerisis**, e.g. lasagne.
- Some modified starches aren't affected by acidity so can be used to thicken acid foods like low calorie salad dressings.

Emulsions
Edexcel • AQA

Liquids that will not mix together are **immiscible**, e.g. oil and water. When shaken together they form an unstable **emulsion**, which separates if left standing. A mixture only remains stable if an emulsifier is used, e.g. **lecithin** in egg yolk is an emulsifier.

Egg yolk is used in the preparation of mayonnaise, where it holds oil and vinegar together. It helps the fat in cakes mix with the egg white.

Foams
Edexcel • AQA

Foams are gas mixed into a liquid giving a light texture, e.g. ice cream. Meringues are a foam made by whisking air (gas) into egg white (liquid).

When you bake them the air expands and the egg white coagulates to give a solid structure.

Quick Test

1. Solutions separate when left to stand.
   True or **false**?
2. What is formed when solids don't mix in a liquid?
3. Which ingredients form the gel in white sauce?
4. What do pre-gelatinised starches do instantly?
5. What is the reason for using egg yolk in mayonnaise?
6. A foam is made by mixing liquid into liquid.
   True or **false**?

KEY WORDS
Make sure you understand these words before moving on!
- Solution
- Suspension
- Gel
- Gelatinisation
- Modified starches
- Smart starches
- Synerisis
- Immiscible
- Emulsion
- Lecithin
- Foams

Functional Properties of Food

Elasticity

Wheat contains two proteins: **glutenin** and **gliadin**. When water is added to wheat flour they form gluten.

Gluten is very stretchy or 'elastic' (it has elasticity). It allows food made from wheat flour, e.g. bread and cakes, to rise. No other cereal has this property.

Plasticity

Plasticity describes how fats **change shape** under pressure, such as rubbing in or spreading.

You can easily rub in…
- soft margarine
- butter
- lard.

Oil can't be easily rubbed in.

Plasticity allows fat to coat each flour particle in rubbed-in products, e.g. shortcrust pastry or shortbread.

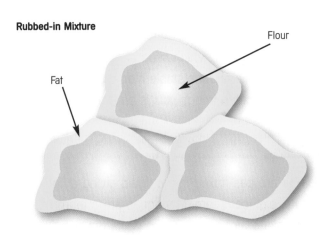

Rubbed-in Mixture

Flour

Fat

Shortening

Fats make cakes and biscuits **crumbly** and 'melt in the mouth' by forming a coating around the starch and protein molecules in the flour. This stops the liquid coming into contact with the flour, and helps stop gluten forming.

Any gluten that does form is in short lengths, not the long elastic strands found in bread. These short gluten strands give us the term shortening.

Effects of Acids and Alkalis on Food

Acids and Food

Edexcel • AQA

Bacteria in milk naturally produce acid by changing the **lactose** to **lactic acid**. This **coagulates** the protein **casein**. The milk becomes lumpy with a sour taste. The lumps are curds and the liquid is called whey. Drained curds are made into cheese.

A similar effect may occur in a recipe using milk and acid, e.g. lemon juice. To prevent this you should thicken the milk with cornflour before adding the acid.

If you add **citric acid** (lemon or lime juice) to cream or condensed milk it coagulates the proteins, giving a thicker consistency, for example key lime pie.

Citric acid also prevents **oxidation**, so you can stop the fruit in a fruit salad from browning by adding lemon or lime juice.

Acetic acid (vinegar) is used because it...

- prevents crystallisation in meringues by changing some of the sucrose to glucose and fructose (invert sugar)
- preserves vegetables, e.g. onions and chutney, by preventing bacterial growth
- gives a sharp flavour, e.g. to salad dressings.

When you're making sauces, acids (e.g. tomatoes, vinegar or lemon juice) break down some of the starch granules. When you're cooking this produces a thinner sauce, so you should allow the sauce to thicken before you add the acid.

Ascorbic acid (Vitamin C) speeds up fermentation in bread making.

Acid pH 1–6

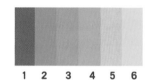

Alkalis and Food

AQA

Alkalis are used as a raising agent, e.g. bicarbonate of soda. When you heat them, they produce sodium carbonate (soda), steam and carbon dioxide.

Cornflour is added to meringues to make a chewy centre.

Alkali pH 8–14

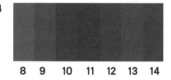

Quick Test

1. What is needed to make gluten?
2. Why are soft margarine and lard good choices for making pastry?
3. The gluten in bread is in short strands. **True** or **false**?
4. What gives key lime pie its thick consistency?
5. Ascorbic acid speeds up fermentation. **True** or **false**?
6. Which acid gives a sharp flavour to salad dressings?

KEY WORDS

Make sure you understand these words before moving on!

- Gluten
- Elasticity
- Plasticity
- Shortening
- Coagulates
- Citric acid
- Acetic acid
- Ascorbic acid
- Alkalis

Raising Agents

Raising Agents

Raising agents work by incorporating a gas into a mixture. When you heat the gases they expand and rise, then escape from the mixture. This gives a light, open texture.

Raising agents may be…
- added by mechanical means, e.g. sieving, beating
- included in the ingredients, e.g. yeast, bicarbonate of soda.

Raising agents are **natural**, e.g. air, steam and yeast, or **chemical**, e.g. bicarbonate of soda, bicarbonate of soda plus an acid, baking powder.

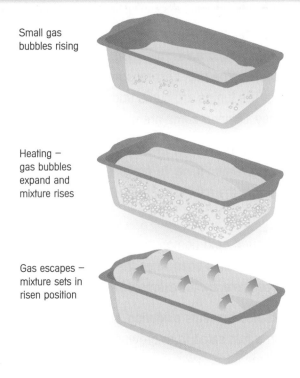

Small gas bubbles rising

Heating – gas bubbles expand and mixture rises

Gas escapes – mixture sets in risen position

Natural Raising Agents

The three gases which make products light are…
- **air**
- **steam**
- **carbon dioxide**.

In most mixtures you use more than one raising agent. For example, if you're making a creamed cake mixture, the main raising agent is the self raising flour, which produces carbon dioxide, but air is incorporated when creaming the butter and sugar.

You **add air mechanically** to food when you're…
- whisking, e.g. in swiss rolls and meringues
- sieving flour, e.g. in cakes and biscuits
- creaming fat and sugar, e.g. in cakes and biscuits
- beating, e.g. in batter and choux pastry
- rubbing in fat to flour, e.g. pastry rubbed in cakes and scones
- rolling and folding, e.g. flaky pastry.

Steam is a raising agent in mixtures with a high proportion of liquid, which are cooked at high temperatures. The water in the mixture turns to steam.

Examples are…
- Yorkshire pudding
- choux pastry
- flaky and rough puff pastry.

It's common to see an open, uneven texture when steam has been a raising agent.

Carbon dioxide is introduced into food using…
- **biological** raising agents, e.g. yeast
- **chemical** raising agents, e.g. bicarbonate of soda.

Biological Raising Agents

Yeast is a micro-organism. When it reproduces it gives off carbon dioxide.

The following conditions are needed for reproduction:

- **Warmth**: most active between **25°C–28°C**. At lower temperatures it reproduces slowly, at high temperatures it is killed.
- **Liquid**.
- **Food**: sugar added to the mixture or obtained from flour.
- **Time**: the mixture must be covered and left to rise in a warm place.

Chemical Raising Agents

Chemical raising agents produce carbon dioxide when they're heated with a liquid:

- **Self raising flour** is convenient to use as it already has the raising agents added.
- **Bicarbonate of soda** (alkali) produces carbon dioxide and washing soda when it's heated. The washing soda is dark yellow with a 'soapy' taste. Bicarbonate of soda is used in cakes with a strong flavour, like gingerbread or parkin, to disguise the soapy taste.

- **Bicarbonate of soda plus an acid**, e.g. sour milk, vinegar, lemon juice or cream of tartar, in other cakes or scones, to prevent the soapy taste.
- **Baking powder** is a mixture of bicarbonate of soda and acid, with a starchy filler to keep it fresh.

Quick Test

1. How can raising agents be added to a mixture?
2. Which three gases make products light?
3. What conditions are needed for yeast to grow?
4. What is baking powder a mixture of?
5. Raising agents make mixtures light. **True** or **false**?

KEY WORDS

Make sure you understand these words before moving on!
- Raising agents
- Carbon dioxide
- Biological
- Chemical

Cooking Food

Why Food is Cooked

Food is cooked to…

- prevent food poisoning, by destroying micro-organisms
- improve its **palatability**, by changing its flavour and texture
- preserve it
- make it easier to digest
- improve the absorption of nutrients
- make it less bulky, e.g. spinach.

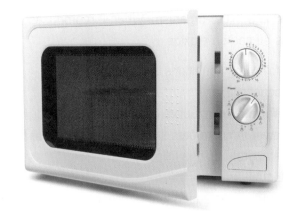

Transferring Heat

Heat transference changes food physically and chemically. Heat can be transferred using wet or dry methods.

You can use a combination of two or all three of the following heat transference methods when you're heating food: **conduction**, **convection** and **radiation**.

In **conduction** the molecules are heated and begin to vibrate faster, colliding with the next molecule and passing on energy. Conduction takes place in a container, e.g. pan, and in the food itself.

Convection takes place in air or liquid. As molecules become hotter they rise, and fall when they cool. In a pan of boiling water, you will see the hot liquid rising and bursting as bubbles on the top. Convection takes place in air in the oven and in water or fat in a pan.

Radiation is the transfer of energy from a heat source, e.g. grill or barbecue, to the food. Radiation waves travel in a straight line to the food. The centre is then heated by conduction. **Microwave** cooking uses a different type of radiation wave, which can travel deeper into the food. Electricity is converted to microwaves by the magnetron. Microwaves travel 5cm into the food. They make the water molecules vibrate, creating friction, which makes heat. **Hot spots** can occur, so you should stir food or leave it to stand before you eat it.

Hob: conduction and convection, e.g. frying, boiling, poaching, stewing, steaming

Grill: radiation and conduction, e.g. grilling, toasting

Oven: conduction and convection, e.g. baking, roasting, casseroling

Making Cakes

Method of Cake Making	Examples
Whisking	Swiss roll, fatless sponge cake
Rubbing in	Scones, raspberry buns, rubbed-in cakes
Melting	Gingerbread
Creaming / All-in-one	Victoria sandwich cake, buns

You can **modify cakes** by...
- using wholemeal flour
- adding flavourings, e.g. lemon zest, dried fruit
- **decorating** their surface
- **enrobing** them with chocolate, icing or marzipan.

Functions of Cake Ingredients

Ingredient	Function
Fat	Flavour; extends shelf life (keeping properties); when margarine is creamed with sugar it traps air, which acts as a raising agent
Sugar	Sweetens; adds colour as the sugar caramelises on heating; softens the structure
Eggs	Trap air to help the mixture rise; act as an emulsifier in creaming and all-in-one cakes; add colour; help form the structure as they coagulate on heating; provide moisture, which converts to steam on heating
Flour	Forms the structure of the cake; dextrinisation of starch gives colour; bulk ingredient

Aeration

Aeration means incorporating air in the mixture. This happens in different ways, depending on the method used:
- **Creaming** sugar and fat together traps air. All-in-one mixtures aren't creamed, so they require extra baking powder to make them rise.
- **Sieving** flour traps air in the flour particles.
- **Whisking** eggs and sugar together traps air.

The air bubbles in the cake are evident in this image.

Pastry

Making Pastry

The table shows the ingredients that are used to make pastry and their functions.

Pastry dishes can be **modified** by altering the **size** and **shape** of the product.

A **finish** is normally applied to pastry products to improve their appearance. You can…

- brush the pastry with egg or milk to give a brown appearance
- sprinkle the pastry with sugar to give an attractive appearance, and to show it's a sweet product.

The pastry lid can be made into a lattice, pinched or forked around the edge. Pastry decoration can be added to the surface. Patterns may be made using a knife or fork.

Ingredient	Function
Flour	• Bulk ingredient • Forms structure • Dextrinisation of starch gives colour
Fat	• Shortens and colours (margarine and butter)
Water	• Binds dry ingredients • Helps form structure • Creates steam to aid rising
Salt	• Flavour

Uses of Pastry

The ratio of ingredients and the way they are combined gives pastry different tastes, textures and appearance:

- **Shortcrust pastry** is used in quiche, jam tarts and lemon meringue pie.
- **Choux pastry** is used in chocolate eclairs and choux buns.
- **Flaky / rough puff pastry** is used in sausage rolls, vanilla slices and pie tops.
- **Suet pastry** is used in steak and kidney pudding and jam roly-poly.
- **Filo pastry** is used in baklava, spring rolls and samosas.
- **Hot water crust pastry** is used in pork pie and game pie.

Choux Pastry

Ready Made Pastry

Ready made pastry includes shortcrust, flaky / rough puff and filo. These may be frozen or chilled.

You can also buy shortcrust pastry mix.

The table shows the advantages and disadvantages of ready made pastry.

Advantages	Disadvantages
• Quick to use • Guaranteed quality • Reliable outcome	• More expensive to buy • May contain additives • Has to be stored until needed

Main Ingredients in Bread

Strong Plain Flour
- bulk ingredient
- forms framework
- gluten allows dough to stretch on rising
- dextrinisation of starch gives colour.

Salt
- flavour
- helps development of gluten.

Yeast
- gives off carbon dioxide, which makes bread rise.

Water
- binds dry ingredients
- helps gluten develop
- helps yeast ferment.

Modifying Bread

You can **modify** basic bread dough by…
- altering the type of flour
- adding other ingredients.

Modification	Effect
Use wholemeal flour instead of strong plain flour	Increases NSP (fibre); taste, texture and appearance are altered
Add cheese	Alters taste and appearance; increases protein and fat content
Add sundried tomatoes, herbs or onions	Affects taste, texture, colour and appearance
Add dried fruit	Sweetens bread; increases NSP (fibre); affects appearance and texture

You can alter the appearance, flavour and texture of bread by adding toppings, such as glace icing, poppy seeds and cheese. You can also alter bread by changing its shape and size.

Quick Test

1. Cooking food changes its flavour and texture. **True** or **false**?
2. Where does convection take place?
3. Give three ways of aerating a cake mixture.
4. Give three functions of flour in pastry.
5. What is the main raising agent in bread?
6. Bread products can be sweet and savoury. **True** or **false**?

KEY WORDS
Make sure you understand these words before moving on!
- Conduction
- Convection
- Radiation
- Decorating
- Enrobing
- Aeration
- Shortens
- Shortcrust pastry
- Bulk ingredient
- Carbon dioxide

Sauces

Sauces

The functions of sauces are to add flavour (sweet, e.g. custard, or savoury, e.g. cheese sauce), moisture and nutritive value.

Sauces are liquids that are thickened. They can form part of a dish, e.g. lasagne, or be served with a meal, e.g. gravy. **Sauces** are also **used** in **food products** like lemon meringue pie, strawberry fruit tart.

Sauces can be different thicknesses, depending on how much liquid you use. The three main uses of sauces are **pouring**, **coating** and **binding**.

Thickening Sauces

Many sauces are thickened by gelatinisation of starch. For instance, blended sauces are made with cornflour, e.g. white sauce. **Arrowroot sauce** is also blended and is used on fruit tarts because it's transparent. Sauces made using the roux and all-in-one methods use flour.

During **gelatinisation**, the following takes place:
- Starch particles don't **dissolve** in liquid. Instead they form a **suspension**.
- **Stirring** or agitating the liquid keeps the starch particles **suspended**.
- If the suspension isn't stirred, the particles sink to the bottom and stick together, forming **lumps**.
- When the liquid reaches **60°C**, the starch grains begin to **absorb liquid** and **swell**.

- At **80°C** the particles **break open** and release starch, making the mixture **thick** and **viscous**. This is **gelatinisation**.
- Gelatinisation is completed when the liquid reaches **100°C**. The thickened liquid now forms a **gel**. On cooling the gel **solidifies**.

Other methods of thickening sauces include...
- **coagulating egg protein**, e.g. egg custard
- **emulsification**, e.g. mayonnaise
- **pureeing**, e.g. raspberry coulis
- **gelatine**, e.g. glaze on flans.

Synerisis happens when proteins are overcooked. They carry on coagulating and squeeze out fat and water. Synerisis can be seen as a thin liquid that has separated from a sauce. To stop this happening manufacturers use modified starch.

Modifying Sauces

One way of modifying a sauce is to **substitute semi-skimmed milk** for **full fat milk**. This alters the **nutritional value** of the sauce, and is useful if you are following a **reduced fat diet**.

You can also add the following ingredients to a sauce:
- **parsley**, to add flavour and colour
- **onion**, to add flavour and texture
- **sugar**, to add sweetness
- **cheese**, to add flavour and enrich the sauce; **red cheese** adds colour
- **chocolate**, to add flavour and colour.

Modifying a Basic Recipe

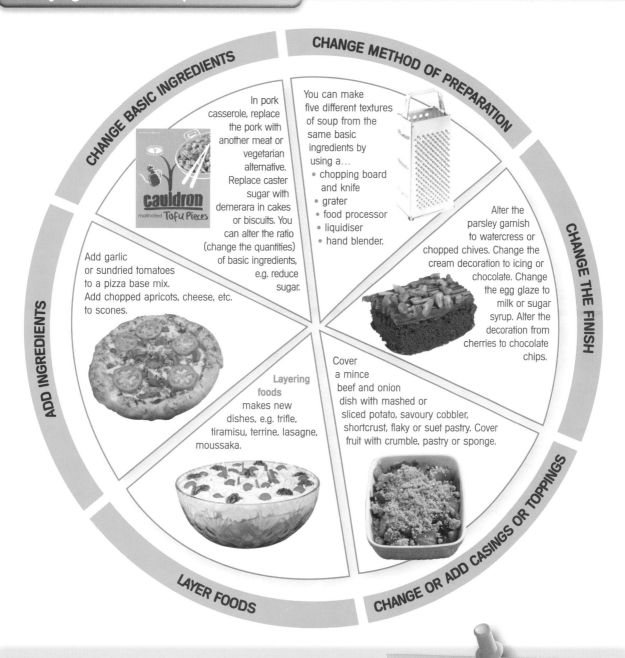

CHANGE BASIC INGREDIENTS

In pork casserole, replace the pork with another meat or vegetarian alternative. Replace caster sugar with demerara in cakes or biscuits. You can alter the ratio (change the quantities) of basic ingredients, e.g. reduce sugar.

CHANGE METHOD OF PREPARATION

You can make five different textures of soup from the same basic ingredients by using a…
• chopping board and knife
• grater
• food processor
• liquidiser
• hand blender.

CHANGE THE FINISH

Alter the parsley garnish to watercress or chopped chives. Change the cream decoration to icing or chocolate. Change the egg glaze to milk or sugar syrup. Alter the decoration from cherries to chocolate chips.

CHANGE OR ADD CASINGS OR TOPPINGS

Cover a mince beef and onion dish with mashed or sliced potato, savoury cobbler, shortcrust, flaky or suet pastry. Cover fruit with crumble, pastry or sponge.

LAYER FOODS

Layering foods makes new dishes, e.g. trifle, tiramisu, terrine, lasagne, moussaka.

ADD INGREDIENTS

Add garlic or sundried tomatoes to a pizza base mix. Add chopped apricots, cheese, etc. to scones.

Quick Test

1. List three reasons for using sauces.
2. Starch particles don't dissolve. **True** or **false**?
3. At what temperature do starch grains begin to absorb liquid and swell?
4. Spaghetti bolognaise is a layered product. **True** or **false**?

KEY WORDS

Make sure you understand these words before moving on!
• Gelatinisation
• Blended sauces
• Roux
• Synerisis
• Layering foods

Practice Questions

1 Fill in the missing words to complete the following sentences.

Some modified starches allow food to be reheated without _____. Some modified

starches are _____, so they thicken instantly. Some modified starches aren't affected

by _____, so can be used to thicken foods like low calorie salad dressings.

2 Choose the correct words from the options given to complete the following sentences.

dissolved   **solid**   **gas**   **suspension**   **emulsifier**

Foams are _____ mixed into a liquid. A mixture of oil and water only remains stable if

an _____ is used. A solution is a liquid _____ in another liquid.

A _____ is formed when solid particles are added to liquid but don't dissolve.

A gel is a _____ jelly-like substance.

3 Which of these sentences describe the function of acetic acid (vinegar)? Tick the correct options.

A Acetic acid gives a sharp flavour to salad dressings. ◯

B Acetic acid acts as an emulsifier in mayonnaise. ◯

C Acetic acid preserves vegetables by preventing bacterial growth. ◯

D Acetic acid speeds up fermentation in bread making. ◯

E Acetic acid prevents crystallisation in meringues. ◯

4 Explain briefly how raising agents work.

_____

_____

_____

5 Which three gases are used to make products light?

a) _____

b) _____

c) _____

Collins Revision

GCSE
D&T Food Technology
ESSENTIALS

About this Guide

The new GCSE Design & Technology courses are assessed through…
- written exam papers
- controlled assessment.

This guide provides…
- an overview of how your course is assessed
- an explanation of controlled assessment
- advice on how best to demonstrate your knowledge and skills in the controlled assessment.

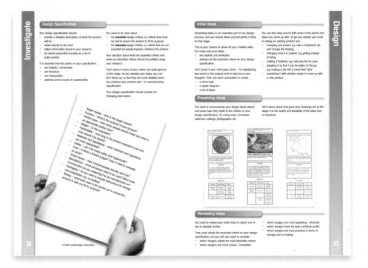

What is Controlled Assessment?

Controlled assessment has replaced coursework. It involves completing a 'design and make' task (two separate tasks for OCR) within a set number of hours.

Your exam board will provide you with a range of tasks to choose from. The purpose of the task(s) is to see how well you can bring all your skills and knowledge together to design and make an original product.

You must produce individual work under controlled conditions, i.e. under the supervision of a teacher.

Your teacher can review your work and give you general feedback, but all the work must be your own.

How is Controlled Assessment Marked?

Your teacher will mark your work using guidelines from the exam board. A moderator at the exam board will review these marks to ensure that they are fair.

You will not just be marked on the quality of your end product - the other stages of design and development are just as important, if not more so!

This means that it is essential to clearly communicate what you did, how you did it, and why you did it, at each stage of the task(s). You will be marked on the quality of your communication too.

Contents

This guide looks at the main stages you will need to go through in your controlled assessment task(s), providing helpful advice and tips along the way:

AQA Design & Technology

Written Paper	2 hours; 120 marks; 40% of total marks
	Section A (30 marks) – A design question based on a context that you will be notified of before the exam.
	Section B (90 marks) – Covers all the content on the specification, i.e. all the material covered in your Essentials Revision Guide.
Controlled Assessment	Approx. 45 hours; 90 marks; 60% of total marks

Edexcel Design & Technology

Written Paper	1 hour 30 minutes; 80 marks; 40% of total marks
Controlled Assessment	Approx. 40 hours; 100 marks (50 for designing and 50 for making); 60% of total marks
	The design and make activities can be linked (combined design and make) or separate (design one product, make another).

OCR Design & Technology

Controlled Assessment: Introduction to Designing & Making	20 hours; 60 marks; 30% of total marks*
Written Paper: Sustainable Design	1 hour; 60 marks; 20% of total marks
	Section A – 15 multiple choice questions.
	Section B – 3 questions requiring short written answers, sketches and annotations.
Controlled Assessment: Making Quality Products	20 hours; 60 marks; 30% of total marks*
	Work for OCR controlled assessments can be submitted on paper (secured in a portfolio or using treasury tags) or as digital files.
Written Paper: Technical Aspects of Designing and Making	1 hour 15 minutes; 60 marks; 20% of total marks
	Section A – 3 questions based on the technical aspects of working with materials, tools and equipment.
	Section B – 2 questions on the design of products reflecting the wider aspects of sustainability and human use. One of these questions will require a design response.

2

Important Considerations

Unlike your teacher, the moderator will not have the opportunity to see how you progress with the task. They will not be able to talk to you or ask questions – they must make their assessment based on the evidence you provide. This means that it is essential to communicate your thoughts, ideas and decisions clearly at each stage of the process:

- Organise your folder so the work is in a logical order.
- Only include information that is relevant.
- Ensure that text is legible and that spelling, punctuation and grammar are accurate.
- Use an appropriate form and style of writing.
- Make sure you use technical terms correctly.

Marks are awarded for quality of presentation but there are more marks available for the content, so make good use of your time – don't waste time creating elaborate borders and titles!

Because you only have a limited amount of time, it is essential to plan ahead. Below are suggested times for each of the stages. These are guidelines only and will vary depending on the total amount of time your exam board allows for the task(s) (see p.2).

Investigate	Analysing the brief	1 hour
	Research	2–3 hours
	Design specification	1 hour
Design	Initial ideas	5–6 hours
	Review	1 hour
Develop	Development	5–6 hours
	Product specification	1-2 hours
Plan	Production Plan	1–2 hours
Make	Manufacture	16 hours
Test and evaluate	Testing and evaluation	1–2 hours

A time plan like this will ensure that you spend a majority of your time on the stages that are worth the most marks. It doesn't mean that the other areas aren't important, but quality rather than quantity is the key.

At the end of the controlled assessment you will need to submit a photo of the final product along with a concise design folder. You should aim to produce about 20 x A3 sheets (or 40 x A4 sheets) for your folder (10 x A3 sheets for a short course or for separate design and make tasks).

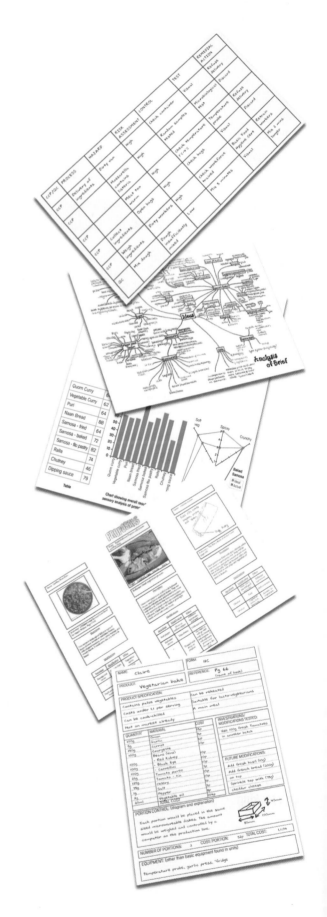

Analysing the Task

To get the most marks, you need to...
- analyse the task / brief in detail
- clearly identify all the design needs.

It is a good idea to start by...
- writing out the task / brief as it is written by the exam board
- underlining any words that you don't fully understand
- finding out the meaning of any underlined words
- writing out the brief in your own words (to clarify what you're being asked to do).

You then need to identify any specific issues that must be considered before you can start designing the product.

Ask yourself the following questions:
- Who will use the end product?
- What will it be used for?
- Where will it be used?
- What sort of shop/retail outlet will it be sold through?
- Are there any cost restrictions that will influence my design?
- How many products would be made if it went into commercial production?

Make sure you have clear answers to all the above before you go any further.

You don't need to write an essay. You could use...
- an attribute analysis table
- a mind map
- a spider diagram
- a list of bullet points.

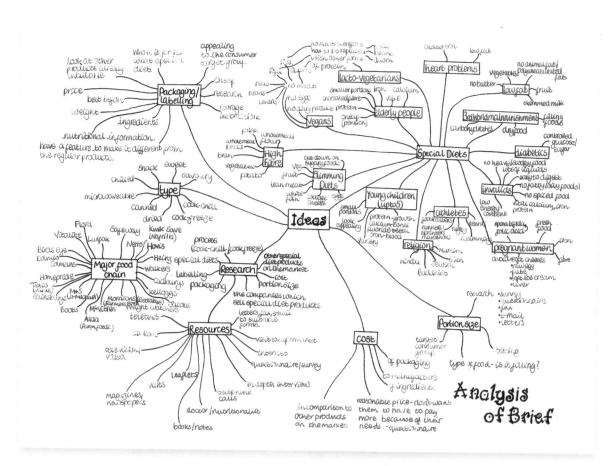

Research

Because you don't have very long to conduct your research, you need to make sure it is all relevant. It should help you to make decisions about all the issues that you identified in your task analysis, so these are the areas to focus on.

Make sure you keep accurate records. You will need to refer back to them throughout the task.

You should know about the different research methods used in the food industry, but be aware that they may not be appropriate to your design task because of the limited time available to you. Possibly the most useful types of research that you can carry out are…

- a questionnaire to find out about the target market / consumer
- sensory analysis of existing products
- disassembly of existing products.

Product Analysis

By taking apart existing food products you can find out what they contain and how they were made. This is called disassembly. You should look at…

- what ingredients have been used and why – try to list all the ingredients and identify why they were used
- the functionality of the product – does it do what it is supposed to do?
- the suitability of the product – is it appropriate for the target market?
- the ergonomics of the product / packaging – has it been designed to make it safer, easier and more efficient to eat / use?
- how the product was manufactured – can you easily identify all the processes that were used?
- the nutritional value of the product – is the product as healthy as it could be?
- factors that will have influenced the product – is it affected by health issues or environmental factors?
- what storage and preparation is required – how should it be stored and does it need to be reheated?
- what the packaging is like – does the packaging have any special features, does it protect the product and what does it say about the product?
- what the costs involved were – how much would it cost to make and how much is it being sold for?

You should also perform sensory analysis to identify where improvements can be made to an existing product's appearance / visual appeal, taste, touch / texture, smell and sound, e.g. crunch or fizz (see p.74 of the Essentials Revision Guide).

As part of your product analysis you might also want to get feedback from consumers:

- What do they like about it?
- What don't they like about it?
- Is it good value for money?
- What improvements would they like to see made?

The purpose of product analysis is to help you produce a product that is better than those already available. It should help you to identify…

- desirable / successful features (features you could incorporate into your design)
- undesirable / unsuccessful features (features to avoid in your design)
- areas for improvement (areas that you should try to improve upon in your design, e.g. reducing cost, improving taste).

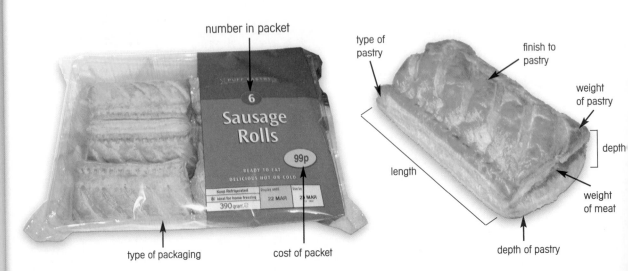

number in packet

type of packaging

cost of packet

type of pastry

finish to pastry

weight of pastry

length

depth

weight of meat

depth of pastry

Interviews, Questionnaires and Surveys

Interviews, questionnaires and surveys normally rely on a large sample group to produce reliable data.

It is fine to adopt these methods for your task - targeting a small, specific group or individual and producing an end product that meets their particular needs - as long as you show that you understand the pros and cons of doing this in your evaluation.

Testing

Make sure tests are useful and relevant and always ensure that they are fair, e.g. test different variables under the same conditions.

Consider testing...
- the effect of using different ingredients
- the effect of changing ratios of ingredients

- different methods of storage and re-heating
- different finishes
- methods of packaging and serving.

Photographs and notes will help to show the moderator what you did.

Research Summary

It is essential to summarise your conclusions and explain how the data gathered through your research will assist you. You should record...
- what you did
- why you did it
- what you hoped to find out (what your expectations were)
- what you actually found out
- how these findings will affect your design ideas.

Information gathered in surveys and questionnaires can be summarised clearly using charts and graphs, but they must be accompanied by an explanation of what the data means – a graph on its own is meaningless!

Star profiles are a great way of comparing different materials and products.

Make sure you list all other sources that you have used, e.g. website, books and in a bibliography.

Dish	Score
Samosa - fried	64
Samosa - baked	72
Samosa - filo pastry	82

Table

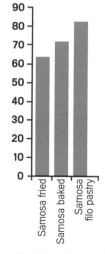

Chart showing overall results from sensory analysis of prototype dishes.

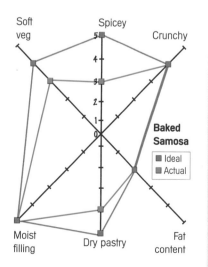

Star profile (radar graph) showing comparison of samosa.

Design Specification

Your design specification should...

- provide a detailed description of what the product will do
- relate directly to the brief
- reflect information found in your research
- be clearly presented (usually as a list of bullet points).

It is essential that the points on your specification...

- are realistic / achievable
- are technical
- are measurable
- address some issues of sustainability.

You need to be clear about...

- the **essential** design criteria, i.e. criteria that must be met to ensure the product is fit for purpose
- the **desirable** design criteria, i.e. criteria that are not essential but would improve / enhance the product.

Your decision about what are essential criteria and what are desirable criteria should be justified using your research.

Don't worry if some of your criteria are quite general at this stage. As you develop your ideas, you can firm these up, so that they are more detailed when you produce your product and / or manufacturing specification.

Your design specification should include the following information:

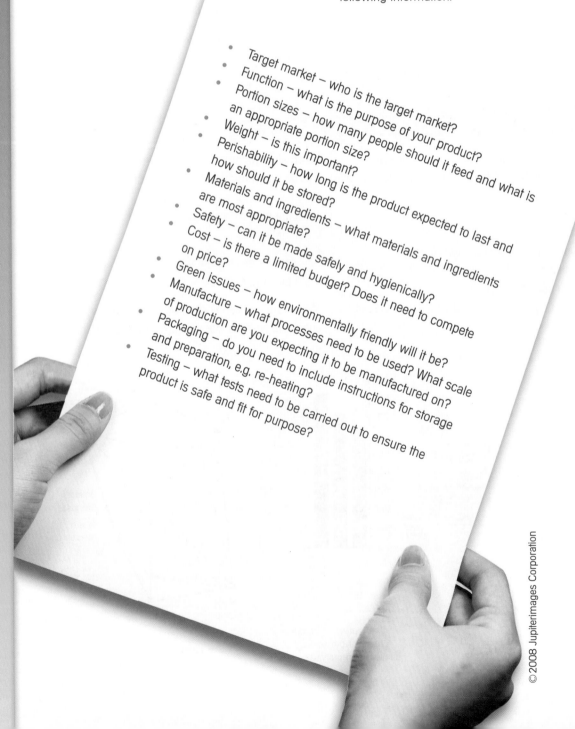

- Target market – who is the target market?
- Function – what is the purpose of your product?
- Portion sizes – how many people should it feed and what is an appropriate portion size?
- Weight – is this important?
- Perishability – how long is the product expected to last and how should it be stored?
- Materials and ingredients – what materials and ingredients are most appropriate?
- Safety – can it be made safely and hygienically?
- Cost – is there a limited budget? Does it need to compete on price?
- Green issues – how environmentally friendly will it be?
- Manufacture – what processes need to be used? What scale of production are you expecting it to be manufactured on?
- Packaging – do you need to include instructions for storage and preparation, e.g. re-heating?
- Testing – what tests need to be carried out to ensure the product is safe and fit for purpose?

Initial Ideas

Generating ideas is an important part of any design process, and you should allow yourself plenty of time for this stage.

This is your chance to show off your creative skills, but make sure your ideas...
- are realistic and workable
- address all the essential criteria on your design specification.

Don't panic if your mind goes blank – try highlighting key words in the original brief to help focus your thoughts. Then use word association to create...
- a mind map
- a spider diagram
- a list of ideas.

You can then play around with some of the words and ideas you came up with. To get you started, you could try taking an existing product and...
- changing one aspect, e.g. take a shepherds pie and change the topping
- changing how it is cooked, e.g. grilling instead of frying
- making it healthier, e.g. reducing the fat used
- adapting it so that it can be eaten on the go, e.g. making a pie into a hand-held 'slice'
- combining it with another recipe to come up with a new product.

Presenting Ideas

You need to communicate your design ideas clearly and show how they relate to the criteria on your design specification. Try using notes, annotated sketches, cuttings, photographs, etc.

Don't worry about how good your drawings are at this stage; it is the variety and feasibility of the ideas that is important.

Name: Cowboy Bean Bake

Reference: 'Children's step-by-step Cook Book' by Angela Wilkes. Page 62-63.

Description

This recipe is made out of different types of beans (haricot, borlotti or red kidney beans), with chopped tomatoes, onion, spicy sausage and streaky bacon. I would serve this in a dish with bread.

Modifications

Ingredient	Modification	Effect
Sausage and bacon	Exclude from recipe.	Vegetarian option
-	Serve in a jacket potato.	More substantial meal.
Fresh cooked beans	Baked beans	Different taste and appearance.

Name: Roast Halloumi Peppers with Lemon and Pine Nuts.

Pepper halloumi cheese Pine nuts thyme

Reference: Greek yoghurt recipe cards.

Description

These roast peppers are stuffed with halloumi cheese, mint leaves and fresh thyme. They are scattered with pine nuts and roasted in the oven with olive oil. I think that these roast peppers will appeal to people as they are something a bit different. I think they will make a good light lunch served with crusty bread.

Modifications

Ingredient	Modification	Effect
Red pepper	Green or yellow pepper	Different appearance and taste.
Halloumi cheese	Feta cheese	Different taste
-	Topped with strips of chicken	The chicken will go well with the lemon and oregano. It will add more protein and flavour to the dish.

Name: Chicken Parcels

Filled with cooked chicken, onions and spices.

Puff Pastry

Reference: 'The Diary Book of British Food.' page 160.

Description

These pasties are filled with spicy chicken, onion and carrot in a puff pastry case. They will be easy to serve and can be warmed up and eaten hot or left cold. They can be eaten with a side salad (cold) or with chips and vegetables (if pasty is heated).

Modifications

Ingredient	Modification	Effect
-	Made into a pie with puff pastry top.	Different appearance.
Chicken	Pork	Different taste.
Chicken	Vegetables (peas, leek, potato etc.)	Suitable for vegetarians.

Reviewing Ideas

You need to review your initial ideas to select one or two to develop further.

They must satisfy the essential criteria on your design specification, but you will also want to consider...
- which designs satisfy the most desirable criteria
- which designs are most unique / innovative
- which designs are most appealing / attractive
- which designs have the best nutritional profile
- which designs are most practical in terms of storage and re-heating.

Developing Ideas

Your aim at the development stage is to modify and revise your initial idea(s) until you reach the best possible design solution.

When your teacher and the moderator look at the end product and your development sheets they will expect to see a design that is much improved compared to your initial idea.

At this stage, you need to use your knowledge of a wide range of materials, ingredients and processes. Your work should show a good understanding of…
- properties of materials and ingredients
- the advantages / disadvantages of materials and ingredients
- the advantages / disadvantages of different processes
- social, moral, environmental and sustainability issues that are relevant to your product.

This means you must select the most appropriate materials, components and manufacturing processes for your product and justify your choices.

Now is a good time to seek other people's opinions, especially if you consulted them at the research stage. Their feedback should help you to make any necessary modifications.

At the end of this process you should have enough information to produce a detailed product specification and / or manufacturing specification.

Once you feel that you have reached the best possible design solution, make sure it is presented in a way that someone else can understand.

Modelling

Making samples (i.e. modelling) is an important part of the development process in Food Technology. It allows you to…
- check that your designs work in practice
- modify and improve your initial designs
- trial a variety of suitable making methods and techniques.

You could…
- model the original recipe, then change one ingredient and model it again, e.g. change white flour to wholemeal flour
- compare the nutritional profile of different modifications
- model different methods of cooking, preparation and assembly
- model different ratios of ingredients, e.g. adjust the

ratio of flour to fat in pastry, or adjust the ratio of filling to pastry in a pie.

Depending on the size and cost of your end product, you may choose to produce full-size samples or scale down your recipe to produce smaller samples.

You must apply the same standards of hygiene and safety when you prepare food samples, as you would for the end product.

Tests are also important to ensure that your final design meets all the essential criteria on your design specification. This should include sensory analysis of all the samples you produce.

Pastry Recipe

125g plain flour
55g butter
pinch of salt
30-45ml cold water

	Ratio	Flour	Weight Butter
Control	70 : 30	125g	55g
Test 1	50 : 50	90g	90g
Test 2	60 : 40	110g	70g
Test 3	80 : 20	145g	35g

Using ICT

You should use of a **range** of communication techniques and media, including ICT and Computer Aided Design (CAD), where appropriate, throughout the design and make task(s). This is particularly important at the development stage.

This can include...
- standard applications, like Word or Excel
- specialist software, e.g. for nutritional analysis
- digital camera
- scanner
- plotter / cutter
- CAM.

Software that can be used for CAD keeps developing and improving. If it is available to you and it is appropriate, you should try to use some CAD for at least part of your final design.

You might use specialist software to...
- make templates
- improve the accuracy and clarity of your drawings
- create numerical data for use on CNC machinery.

© 2008 Jupiterimages Corporation

Product Specification

Your product specification will be more detailed than your design specification.

It will include...
- a list of materials and ingredients
- quantities needed and estimated costs
- a list of tools and equipment required
- technical details about the processes and techniques required
- information about packaging, storage, shelf-life and reheating
- details of size / dimensions (with working drawings or a diagram)
- information about ingredients that may trigger allergic reactions.

You should use your product specification to build and test a prototype of your end product.

Having made the prototype, you can refine this document along with your working drawings and production plan to produce the manufacturing specification, i.e. a comprehensive set of instructions that a third party could use to manufacture your product.

It is essential that you can justify everything that is included in any of your specifications, i.e. you must explain why you chose those particular ingredients, tools, processes, etc. and rejected others.

NAME: Claire	FORM: 11C
PRODUCT: Vegetarian bake	REFERENCE: Pg 66 (name of book)

PRODUCT SPECIFICATION:

Contains pulse vegetables	Can be reheated
Costs under £1 per serving	Suitable for lacto-vegetarians
Can be cook-chilled	A main meal
Not on market already	

QUANTITY	MATERIAL	COST	INVESTIGATIONS/ MODIFICATIONS TESTED:
100g	Onion	15p	
5g	Garlic	5p	Use 100g fresh Tomatoes
150g	Carrot	6p	in another batch
100g	Courgette	10p	
	Beans (tins)		
100g	- Red Kidney	10p	
100g	- Black Eye	10p	
100g	- Cannellini	10p	FUTURE MODIFICATIONS:
25g	Tomato puree	7p	
125g	Tomato - tin	10p	Add fresh basil (10g)
75g	celery	10p	Add french bread (200g)
1g	Salt	1p	on top
2g	Pepper	2p	Sprinkle top with (75g)
20ml	Vegetable oil	8p	cheddar cheese
	TOTAL COST	104p	

PORTION CONTROL: (diagram and explanation)

Each portion would be placed in the same sized microwaveable dishes. The amount would be weighed and controlled by a computer on the production line.

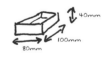

NUMBER OF PORTIONS: 2	COST/PORTION: 52p	TOTAL COST: £1.04

EQUIPMENT: (other than basic equipment found in units)

Temperature probe, garlic press, 'fridge

Production Plan

Your production plan should show…

- the different stages of manufacture in the correct order
- when and what quality control checks will take place
- where the critical control points are.

A flow chart might be the best way of presenting your production plan although sometimes a simple chart listing the stages and the equipment that will be used is equally suitable.

1. Peel vegetables

2. Dice vegetables

3. Control check: size of dice

4. Cook vegetables with spice

5. Control check: are vegetables cooked?

6. Prepare pastry

If you draw a flow chart, there are different, specific symbols for each stage of the process. Some are shown here:

Terminator — Start or end of the system

Process — The activity to be carried out

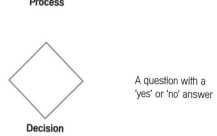

Decision — A question with a 'yes' or 'no' answer

The symbols are linked together by arrows to show the correct sequence of events.

You should aim to keep your flow chart as clear and simple as possible.

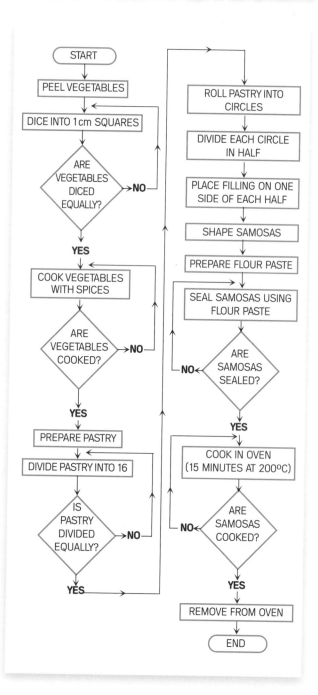

Manufacture

Your revision guide includes information on many of the materials, tools, processes and methods relevant to your particular subject.

In making the prototype of your final product you should demonstrate that, for each specific task, you can select and use...
- appropriate tools and equipment
- appropriate processes, methods and techniques (including CAM where relevant)
- appropriate materials
- appropriate hygiene techniques
- all the above correctly and safely.

You should aim to demonstrate a wide range of skills and processes with precision and accuracy.

Remember, all the materials, methods and processes that you choose must help to make your product the best possible design solution for the brief. Don't include something just to show off your skills!

The finished product should be...
- skillfully and accurately made
- well finished
- edible.

Don't worry if it doesn't turn out quite the way you hoped though - you will earn marks for all the skills and processes you demonstrate, so make sure you record them all clearly in your folder.

For each stage of production, make sure you include...
- a list and / or photograph of materials and ingredients used
- a list and / or photograph of tools and equipment used
- a flow chart / step-by-step description of the process carried out
- an explanation of any safety measures you had to take.

You can use photographs to create a pictorial flow chart to show the moderator the making process from start to finish.

You must include a photograph of the end product and it is a good idea to include photographs of the various stages of making too.

Health and Safety

Before you begin making your product, always carry out a risk assessment.

Look at each stage of your production plan in turn and make a list of possible health and safety risks.

Work back through the list and plan how you will minimize the risks at each stage, e.g. by wearing the correct protective clothing, by ensuring you know how to use the tools correctly, etc.

Make sure you include a HACCP chart in your flowchart or as part of your production plan (see p.85 of the Essentials Revision Guide).

Industry

You should have a good understanding of the methods and processes used in the design and manufacturing industries in your subject area.

Although you will probably only produce one final product, it is important to show that you are aware of various possible methods of production and how your product would be manufactured commercially. You should explain this in your project folder.

If your product could potentially be manufactured using several different methods, try to list the pros and cons for each method and then use these lists to make a decision about which method you would recommend.

If you know that a method or process you are using to make your product would be carried out differently in a factory, make a note of this in your project folder – this will show your teacher and moderator how much you know!

Quality Control and Assurance

Your revision guide looks at some of the quality control tests and quality assurance checks used in industry that are relevant to your particular subject.

You may be able to apply some to your own product.

Even if you can't, you should still identify and explain the ones that would be relevant to your product if it were to be produced commercially.

Remember to include drawings of any relevant quality assurance symbols.

The quality checks you need to make throughout the manufacturing stages should also be included in your flowchart or production plan. It is also important to show any modifications needed to improve the quality of the product.

Part of a HACCP Chart

CCP/QC	PROCESS	HAZARD	RISK ASSESSMENT	CONTROL	TEST	REMEDIAL ACTION
CCP	Delivery of ingredients	Dirty van	High	Check container	Visual	Refuse delivery
CCP		Mozzarella contains listeria	High	Random samples tested	Microbiological test	Discard
CCP		Meat too warm	High	Check temperature 1°C-4°C	Temperature probe	Refuse delivery
CCP	Collect ingredients	Open bags	High	Check bags	Visual	Discard
CCP	Weigh ingredients	Dirty workers	High	Check workforce trained	Basic Food Hygiene cert	Retrain workers
QC	Mix dough	Dough insufficiently mixed	Low	Mix 5 minutes	Visual	Mix 2 mins longer

All elements of your final product need to be tested to ensure that they meet the original design criteria.

A **range** of tests should be carried out to check the performance and / or quality of the final product, but you need to justify each test you carry out, i.e. explain why it is important.

Tests do not have to be complicated. They just need to be sensible and helpful, e.g. carry out consumer taste tests.

Different types of test are covered on p.75 of your Essentials Revision Guide.

Keeping records is very important. In your project folder you need to explain...
- what tests were carried out
- why the tests were carried out
- what you found out
- what modifications you would make based on the test results.

Makes sure you take photos of your product before testing begins, so that you have a record of what it looked like.

© University of Abertay Dundee

Please place a tick (✓) in the appropriate box for each sample, where:
1 = dislike a lot
2 = dislike
3 = neither like or dislike
4 = like
5 = like a lot

Sample	1	2	3	4	5
35642					
87694					
98076					
42318					

Evaluation

The final evaluation should summarise all your earlier conclusions (from research and reviews) and provide an objective evaluation of the final prototype.

It should refer to the criteria on your original design specification directly.

When carrying out an evaluation, you should ask yourself the following questions:

- Does the product meet all the criteria on the original brief / specification?
- Is the product easy to store and re-heat?
- Does the product look, taste and smell the way it was intended to?
- Do you like / dislike any features? Explain why.
- Would you purchase the product and what would you be prepared to pay for it?
- What are its advantages and disadvantages compared to similar products?
- What impact does making and using the product have on the environment?
- Can it be made for a fair price?

It is important to ask these questions of end-users too!

Depending on the answers to these questions, you can include suggestions for further modifications in your evaluation.

Honesty is the best policy when writing evaluations. If something didn't work, say so – but always suggest a way of preventing the same problem in future.

6 Which gas is used to make each of the following products rise? Tick the correct options.

A Swiss roll Air ◯ Steam ◯ CO_2 ◯

B Bread Air ◯ Steam ◯ CO_2 ◯

C Yorkshire pudding Air ◯ Steam ◯ CO_2 ◯

D Scones Air ◯ Steam ◯ CO_2 ◯

E Creamed cakes Air ◯ Steam ◯ CO_2 ◯

7 Which of these methods adds air mechanically to food? Tick the correct options.

A Creaming ◯

B Baking ◯

C Sieving ◯

D Rolling and folding ◯

E Cutting ◯

F Rubbing in ◯

G Beating ◯

H Whisking ◯

8 Fill in the missing words to complete the following sentence.

The conditions needed for yeast to grow are ...., ...,

.... and ....

9 Circle the correct options in the following sentences.

a) Strong **plain** / **self raising** flour already contains raising agent.

b) Bicarbonate of soda produces CO_2 and **washing** / **baking** soda.

c) To prevent a soapy taste, bicarbonate of soda is mixed with an **alkali** / **acid**.

10 How is heat transferred to food in the oven? Tick the correct option.

A Conduction and radiation ◯

B Radiation and convection ◯

C Convection and conduction ◯

Enzymes

Controlling Micro-organisms

All foods change over time. These changes are not always harmful, e.g. hanging meat makes it more tender, and the flavour of blue cheese is created by moulds. Food eventually becomes harmful or unpleasant to eat: milk goes sour, fruit becomes mouldy and meat and fish become 'putrid' and can cause food poisoning if you eat them.

To **preserve food**, i.e. make it last longer and extend its shelf life, the **enzymes** and **micro-organisms** (yeasts, moulds and bacteria) that cause these changes must be controlled.

Enzymes

Enzymes are **chemical catalysts** that are found in all cells. They break down plant and animal tissues causing fruit to ripen, meat to tenderise, and oxidation to speed up.

If enzyme activity is allowed to continue, there is food spoilage.

Oxidation or Enzymic Browning

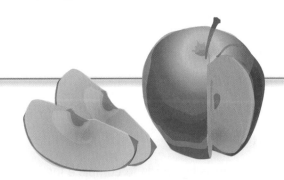

Oxidation (**enzymic browning**) takes place when fruit and vegetables are exposed to air after being cut. This causes the flesh to turn brown.

Ways to Prevent Oxidation (Enzymic Browning)	Example
Adding acid	Add lemon juice to a fruit salad
Blanching	Put carrots into boiling water
Preventing contact with air	Put peeled potatoes into cold water until needed

Quick Test

1. What must be controlled to extend the shelf life of food?
2. Enzymes cause food to ripen. **True** or **false**?
3. What effect does enzymic browning have on fruit?
4. How can you prevent fruit salad turning brown?

KEY WORDS

Make sure you understand these words before moving on!

- Enzymes
- Micro-organisms
- Oxidation
- Enzymic browning
- Blanching

Yeasts

Yeasts...
- are single-celled plants found in the air and on skins of fruit
- spoil the taste of food but don't make it harmful
- grow only on sugary foods
- can survive without air
- can't grow at low temperatures
- can't survive in sugar concentration above 50 per cent
- can't survive in vinegar
- are destroyed by temperatures above 70°C.

To prevent yeasts growing, you should store food at low temperatures. Jams should be made with 60 per cent sugar.

In the food manufacturing industry, yeast **ferments**, and produces alcohol and carbon dioxide given the correct conditions for growth:
- warmth
- moisture
- food
- time.

Yeasts are used to make **bread products**, where the carbon dioxide is used as a raising agent, and **alcoholic drinks**, e.g. beer, wine.

Yeast can be fresh, quick-acting or dried.

Moulds

Moulds are a type of fungus. They...
- settle on food and grow into a visible plant, which resembles coloured fluff
- grow on many foods, including bread, cheese and meat
- like slightly acid conditions
- need moisture
- need warm temperatures between 20°C–40°C
- are destroyed at temperatures above 70°C
- can survive in a fridge, but not a freezer.

Mould on food is a sign that it isn't very fresh or has been badly stored. Some moulds cause allergic reactions and respiratory problems. A few moulds produce poisonous substances, which can make you sick.

In the food manufacturing industry, moulds are used...
- to give the characteristic appearance and flavour to **blue cheese**
- in the production of **Quorn**™.

Bacteria

Bacteria

Bacteria are…

- single-celled organisms that are able to reproduce rapidly
- sometimes harmless and used in making cheese and yoghurt, e.g. probiotic bacteria help digestion
- sometimes harmful (**pathogenic**), and can cause **food poisoning** and even death.

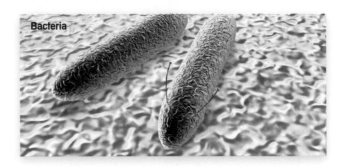

Bacteria

High Risk and Low Risk Foods

Some foods are high risk. This includes foods that aren't cooked before they're eaten. If food is contaminated by bacteria, the bacteria will not be destroyed before the food is eaten.

High risk foods include…

- protein foods, e.g. meat, milk, fish, eggs
- cooked rice and lentils
- moist foods, e.g. gravies and soups
- unpasteurised foods.

Low risk foods include…

- fats and oils
- foods with a high sugar content, e.g. sweets and jams
- high acid content foods, e.g. chutneys and pickles
- foods that are cooked before you eat them.

In food manufacturing, high risk foods are kept separate from raw foods. Workers dealing with raw foods wear different coloured clothing, so they can be seen if they accidentally move to the high risk area of the factory. They must walk through sanitised baths to clean their boots before entering the production area.

Once food is cooked it's kept separate from the raw foods.

Workers in food factories and test kitchens must, by law, make sure that all food is **safe to eat**. You must also produce food safely when you cook at home and school.

Example of a High Risk Food

Example of a Low Risk Food

Food Poisoning Bacteria

Bacteria	Foods Affected	Symptoms	Onset	Special Note
Salmonella	Raw meat, eggs, sea food, dairy products	Diarrhoea, vomiting, fever	12–36 hours	May be fatal to the elderly and babies; found in human and animal excretia
Staphylococcus Aureus	Cooked sliced meat, custards, cream and ice cream	Vomiting, diarrhoea, abdominal pain	1–6 hours	Present in nasal passage, throat and skin; spread by flies
Clostridium perfringens	Raw and cooked meat and meat products	Nausea, diarrhoea, abdominal pain	8–22 hours	N/A
Clostridium Botulinum	Incorrectly canned meat, fish or vegetables	Paralysis, difficulty breathing, double vision, nausea, vomiting	12–48 hours	Rare, often results in death
Bacillus cereus	Cooked rice, pasta and starchy foods, e.g. potatoes	Nausea, vomiting, diarrhoea	1–6 hours	N/A
Escherichia-Coli (E-Coli)	Raw meat, untreated milk and water	Diarrhoea, vomiting, blood in diarrhoea	12–24 hours	Causes gastro enteritis in humans
Listeria Monocytogenes	Soft cheese, pâté, unpasteurised milk, undercooked meat, incorrectly heated cook-chill meals	A range of symptoms from mild flu-like illness to septicaemia, meningitis and pneumonia	No specific time	Can cause miscarriage or premature labour and birth
Campylobacter	Meat, shell fish, untreated water	Diarrhoea, headache, fever, abdominal pain	1–11 days	Easily transmitted between humans

Quick Test

1. All bacteria are harmful. **True** or **false**?
2. Why are probiotic bacteria useful?
3. Are fats and oils high risk or low risk foods?
4. Which food poisoning bacteria causes paralysis?
5. Which bacteria live in our nose and throat?

KEY WORDS
Make sure you understand these words before moving on!
- Yeasts
- Ferments
- Moulds
- Quorn™
- Bacteria
- Pathogenic
- Food poisoning
- High risk
- Low risk

Conditions for Bacterial Growth

Conditions for Bacterial Growth

There are **five main conditions** for bacterial growth:
1. temperature
2. moisture
3. time
4. pH level
5. oxygen.

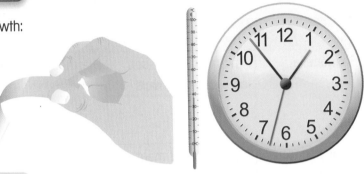

1. Temperature

Bacteria grow best at 37°C, which is body temperature, but they can reproduce quickly at any temperature between 3°C and 63°C. This is known as the **danger zone**.

Cook-chill food should be stored at 0–3°C. The temperature of British chillers is 1–5°C (the World standard is 1–8°C).

To **control** temperature, food should be…
- cooled to below 3°C, or
- heated to above 63°C.

3–63°C
Danger zone

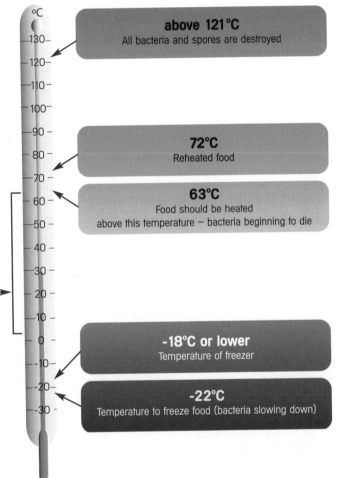

above 121°C
All bacteria and spores are destroyed

72°C
Reheated food

63°C
Food should be heated
above this temperature – bacteria beginning to die

-18°C or lower
Temperature of freezer

-22°C
Temperature to freeze food (bacteria slowing down)

2. Moisture

Bacteria like moist conditions. Many foods have some liquid in them.

Controls for moisture are…
- **dehydration** (drying), which removes the water and prevents bacterial growth, e.g. dried milk powder

- **high sugar content**, which reduces the moisture available, e.g. jam making
- **salt**, which removes water from food by osmosis, e.g. tinned fish, salt for curing bacon
- **freezing**, which turns liquids to solids; this means that moisture isn't available for micro-organisms.

Conditions for Bacterial Growth

3. Time

Bacteria **multiply rapidly**. One bacterium can become one million bacteria in less than seven hours.

To **control** bacteria multiplying, you should…
- eat food soon after it has been made / cooked
- quickly cool food that isn't going to be eaten straight away, and store it in a fridge or freezer.

4. pH Level

Bacteria grow best in a **neutral pH**, between 6.6 and 7.5. They can't survive below pH 4.5.

pH levels are **controlled** by **acidity regulators**, which keep food below pH 4.5.

Vinegar (acetic acid) has a pH of 3.5. It's used to preserve foods, e.g. onions, chutney.

5. Oxygen

Some bacteria, but not all, **require oxygen** in order to reproduce.

To prevent bacteria accessing oxygen, manufacturers **vacuum pack** foods or use a

packaging system that exchanges the air in packaging for other gases. The packaging systems are called **Modified Atmospheric Packaging** (MAP) and **Controlled Atmospheric Packaging** (CAP).

Cross contamination

Food handlers must be very careful not to transfer bacteria from one food to another, to avoid cross contamination.

Cross contamination occurs when…
- raw food touches cooked food, or food that will not be cooked before eating, e.g. cooked meats and salads

- liquid or juices from raw food drips onto high risk food
- hands, knives and / or chopping boards are not washed between preparing raw and cooked foods
- dirty cloths are used to wipe work tops or chopping boards
- dirty towels are used to dry hands.

Quick Test

1. What is the temperature between 3°C and 63°C known as?
2. Bacteria grow most rapidly at 37°C. **True** or **false**?
3. What is the safe temperature range of a fridge?
4. Bacteria need moisture for growth. **True** or **false**?
5. What is the pH level of vinegar?
6. What does MAP stand for?

KEY WORDS

Make sure you understand these words before moving on!
- Temperature
- Moisture
- Time
- pH level
- Oxygen
- Danger zone
- Dehydration
- Acidity regulators
- Cross contamination

Food Hygiene

Personal Hygiene

Working in a **test kitchen** is like working in the Food Technology room at school, or in your own kitchen at home. Every care must be taken to ensure that the food is **safe to eat**.

Throughout food production the home economist will follow a **Hazard Analysis, Critical Control Point** (HACCP) system.

During food production in the test kitchen the home economist will always do the following:

1. Wear a hair net to ensure that no hair can get into the food. A beard and moustache guard must also be worn if necessary.
2. Wash hands thoroughly with an antibacterial cleaner to kill any bacteria on them, and dry hands using a paper towel or hot air dryer.
3. Remove all jewellery when cooking.
4. Cover any cuts with a blue plaster with a metallic strip. This can be easily seen if it falls into food, as few foods are blue. The metallic strip allows the plaster to be identified magnetically.
5. Make sure nails are short and clean. Remove nail polish as it could get into the food.

6. Wear a clean apron or overall (jacket or white coat) to cover clothes.
7. Avoid licking fingers or equipment like spoons.
8. Wash hands after blowing their nose or using the toilet.
9. Avoid picking spots or scabs.

Preparing Food Safely

Wherever food is produced...

- clean equipment and utensils in hot soapy water to kill bacteria (steam is used in industry)
- use **antibacterial cleaner** to clean work surfaces
- use clean dishcloths, tea towels and oven gloves
- store food correctly before, during and after production
- put used equipment near the sink
- throw away rubbish immediately
- use a **probe** to check the temperature of food
- use a clean spoon each time you taste food
- cool food rapidly and store it in the correct conditions
- use the correct colour chopping boards and knives for food preparation.

Colour Coding for Knives and Chopping Boards

white for bakery and dairy products

red for raw meat

blue for raw fish

green for salad and fruits

yellow for cooked meats

brown for raw vegetables

Temperature Probe

Shelf Life

Commercially produced food always has a **shelf life**. This is the amount of time that the food is either safe to eat, or will be in the best condition. When foods like potato crisps or biscuits pass their **sell by date** they're not unsafe to eat, but may not be in the best condition for the consumer to enjoy them.

A wide variety of **preservation methods** and **packaging techniques** are used in food manufacturing to extend the shelf life of foods. Disadvantages of preservation are that the nutritional value is decreased (especially vitamins), the sensory qualities are changed and additives may be used.

Methods of Extending Shelf Life

There are a variety of ways to extend shelf life:

- **Modified Atmospheric Packaging (MAP)** is when food is sealed in a packet. Air is replaced by another gas, which prevents bacterial growth. MAP is used for bacon, smoked fish, and air freighted fruit and vegetables.
- **Vacuum packing** is when air is removed from a sealed packet. This helps food to keep its flavour, e.g. coffee.
- Food labels must always declare irradiation. **Irradiation** isn't the same as radiation. It delays food ripening, e.g. strawberries, stops vegetables sprouting, e.g. potatoes, and destroys small insects found on spices or in cereal.
- **Additives** are chemicals that are added to food.
- **Applying heat**. Micro-organisms are destroyed by high temperatures.

- **Dehydration / drying** removes the moisture in food, so that micro-organisms can't survive. Some foods, such as fruit, tomatoes and spices, are dried by laying them in the sun. In the home, the oven and microwave can be used to dry some fruits and herbs.
- **Reducing temperature**. Low temperatures slow down the growth of bacteria.

Grapes Drying in the Sun; When Dried They will be Raisins

Quick Test

1. Which chopping board should be used for raw meat?
2. What type of plaster should be used on cuts when handling food?
3. Always remove all jewellery when cooking. **True** or **false**?
4. Hands should always be washed after using the lavatory. **True** or **false**?
5. Which method of extending shelf life can stop potatoes sprouting?
6. Which method of extending shelf life slows down the growth of bacteria?

KEY WORDS

Make sure you understand these words before moving on!
- Hazard Analysis, Critical Control Point
- Antibacterial cleaner
- Probe
- Shelf life
- Irradiation
- Additives

Low Temperatures

Low Temperature Methods

Bacteria become **dormant** (don't reproduce, but aren't dead) at low temperatures. Bacteria aren't destroyed by the low temperatures, and when food warms up they become active again.

There are three main ways of keeping food at low temperatures:

- **chilling**
- **cook-chilling**
- **freezing**.

Chilling and Cook-chilling

Chilling is used for foods like sandwiches and cream cakes. The food keeps for a **short time** and is stored between 1°C and 5°C. The low temperature slows down enzyme activity and bacterial growth.

Cook-chilling is used for ready meals. Food is cooked and cooled to 0°C to 3°C in 90 minutes or less. It is stored in a **refrigerator** at 0°C to 3°C. Products have a shelf life of 5 days.

Freezing

Freezing is used for prepared dishes, fruit and vegetables. It can be done commercially or at home.

At home frozen food should be kept at -18°C. **Blanching** may be necessary for some fruit and vegetables before freezing.

Quick freezing reduces cell damage in food. It forms small ice crystals, which reduces damage to cell walls. **Slow freezing** causes big ice crystals, which can break the cell walls. When defrosted, the food will have a poor texture.

In industry, **cryogenic freezing**, using liquid nitrogen, is used to rapidly reduce food to a very low temperature. This minimises cell damage. Commercially, food is kept at a temperature between -18°C and -29°C before being sold.

Frozen food is transported in special vehicles to keep it at the correct temperature.

Quick Freezing

Slow Freezing

Chillers and Freezers

To maintain the temperature of chillers and freezers…

- regularly monitor the temperature with a **probe** or **digital reader** (**data logging**)
- record the temperature, so it can be used as evidence if required by an Environmental Health officer
- use sensors and warning lights to warn of a rise in temperature
- keep doors shut
- check and maintain seals around doors
- defrost regularly
- do not overfill.

Consumer Use

Most **food poisoning** is caused by poor food transportation, storage and use at home. Frozen, chilled and cook-chill foods should be…

- transported home quickly
- stored and cooked according to instructions.

Remember that…

- cook-chill dishes must be eaten within two hours of cooking
- you shouldn't **reheat** leftovers
- you mustn't **refreeze** frozen foods.

Accelerated Freeze Drying

Accelerated freeze drying (AFD) is a combination of **freezing** and **drying**.

Food is quick frozen, and then placed in a **vacuum** under reduced pressure. It's heated and the ice is changed to vapour, leaving the food dry. AFD food is light and easily restored by adding water, e.g. dried soups. The flavour, colour and nutritional value aren't significantly changed. These food products may be kept at ambient (room) temperature.

Quick Test

1. Bacteria are destroyed by low temperatures. **True** or **false**?
2. What is the temperature range of a chiller?
3. How quickly must cook-chill foods be cooled to below 3°C?
4. Who might need to see the evidence of recorded temperatures from freezers and chillers?
5. Left over cook-chill food can be saved and reheated again the next day. **True** or **false**?
6. How are AFD foods restored?

KEY WORDS

Make sure you understand these words before moving on!

- Dormant
- Chilling
- Cook-chilling
- Freezing
- Digital reader
- Accelerated freeze drying

High Temperature Methods

Pasteurisation and UHT

During **pasteurisation** liquid is heated and held at a **high temperature** for a **short time** (HTST). Pasteurisation is mainly used to process milk, fruit juices and other liquids, e.g. soup.

Different liquids are heated to different temperatures for different amounts of time.

Milk is heated to 72°C for 15 seconds, and then cooled rapidly to below 10°C, which extends its shelf life by days. But it only **kills some bacteria**.

During **Ultra Heat-Treatment** (**UHT**), liquid is heated to a **very high temperature** for a **short time** (HTST). Milk is heated to 133°C for 1 second, and this extends shelf life by months. It causes no change to the flavour of the liquid, and **kills all bacteria**.

Pasteurisation of Milk Takes Place in Large Vats

Sterilisation

During **sterilisation**, food is heated to **high temperatures** for longer than pasteurisation or UHT. When sterilising, milk is heated to 110°C and held for 30 minutes, which extends the shelf life by months. In milk the flavour is changed because of the **caramelisation** of lactose (sugar). **Most bacteria are destroyed**.

Canning

Canning is a form of **sterilisation**. Food can be...
- packed in cans or bottles and then sterilised
- sterilised and packed into sterile containers.

The containers are **sealed** to prevent re-contamination.

The advantages of canning are that food...
- has a very long shelf life
- can be kept at **ambient** (room) temperature, without the need for expensive equipment.

Once opened, canned foods should be stored in a different, sealed container in the fridge.

Home preservation

High temperature methods of **home preservation** include making jams, pickles and chutneys.

Additives and E Numbers

Additives may be...

- **natural**, e.g. beetroot juice as a red colouring
- **chemical**, i.e. made by scientists, e.g. aspartame
- **synthetic**, i.e. have the same chemical structure as natural additives but made in a laboratory.

The **E number** indicates that an additive has passed the **European Community Safety Standards**. The E number is a code used instead of a long chemical name, e.g. pentasodium triphosphate is known as E451.

Uses of Additives

Additives are used as...

- **colours** (E100s), e.g. drinks, icing, etc.
- **preservatives** (E200s), which extend shelf life, e.g. sausages and canned meats
- **emulsifiers** and **stabilisers** (E400s). Examples of emulsifiers are lecithin, which lets oil and water mix, e.g. ice cream. Stabilisers stop ingredients separating, e.g. sauces, Xanthan gum
- **antioxidants** (E300s), which prevent oxidation of fats, and slow enzymic browning of fruit and vegetables
- **gelling agents**, which are used to set jams, e.g. E440 (pectin), and change consistency of some foods, e.g. sweets
- **flavour enhancers** (E600s), which make natural flavours stronger, e.g. monosodium glutamate (MSG) (E621), soups, snacks
- **natural flavourings**, which include herbs and spices, e.g. parsley, cinnamon and vanilla

- **flavourings**, which don't have an E number. They are shown as 'flavouring', e.g. strawberry flavouring in cold desserts
- **sweeteners**, which have fewer calories than natural sugar. Intense sweeteners are much sweeter, e.g. aspartame
- **thickeners**, which are used to thicken liquids
- **anti-caking agents**, which prevent dry ingredients sticking together.

Some consumers don't eat food with chemical and synthetic additives, as a life choice. **Hyperactivity** in children has been linked to food colourings, e.g. tartrazine.

Quick Test

1. Pasteurisation kills all the bacteria in milk. **True** or **false**?
2. What does HTST mean?
3. Canning is a form of what?
4. Synthetic additives are found in natural foods. **True** or **false**?
5. Do flavourings have E numbers?

KEY WORDS

Make sure you understand these words before moving on!

- Pasteurisation
- Ultra Heat-Treatment
- Sterilisation
- Canning
- Ambient
- Preservatives
- Emulsifiers
- Stabilisers
- Antioxidants
- Flavour enhancers

Practice Questions

1 Which of the following doesn't prevent oxidation (enzymic browning)? Tick the correct option.

    A   Preventing contact with air ◯   **B**   Adding acid ◯

    C   Freezing ◯   **D**   Blanching ◯

2 Which of the following statements about yeast are correct? Tick the correct options.

    A   Yeast is found in the air. ◯

    B   Yeast is destroyed by temperatures above 55°C. ◯

    C   Yeast makes food mouldy. ◯

    D   Yeast grows at low temperatures. ◯

    E   Yeast can survive without air. ◯

    F   Yeast grows on sugary food. ◯

    G   Yeast spoils the taste of food. ◯

3 Circle the correct options in the following sentences.

    a)   Moulds grow into a **visible** / **invisible** plant.

    b)   Moulds like **alkaline** / **acid** conditions.

    c)   Moulds are destroyed at temperatures above **50°C** / **70°C**.

    d)   Moulds **can** / **can't** survive in a refrigerator.

    e)   Moulds **can** / **can't** survive in a freezer.

4 Choose the correct words from the options given to complete the following sentences.

probiotic   **harmful**   **digestion**   **single**   **rapidly**   **cheese**   **food poisoning**

Bacteria are _____-celled organisms which are able to reproduce

_____. Some are _____ and cause _____

_____ or even death. Some are harmless and used in _____

making. _____ bacteria help _____.

5 Explain how moisture can be controlled to prevent bacteria reproducing.

_____

_____

_____

_____

6 Which of the following statements is true? Tick the correct option.

   A   In MAP air is replaced with another gas.   ◯

   B   Additives don't extend shelf life.   ◯

   C   Dehydration causes bacterial growth.   ◯

   D   Irradiation doesn't delay food ripening.   ◯

7 What is meant by cross contamination?

8 Which of the following statements is true? Tick the correct option.

   A   Bacteria are destroyed by low temperatures.   ◯

   B   Cook-chill products have a shelf life of five days.   ◯

   C   If bacteria are dormant they are dead.   ◯

   D   Frozen food at home should be kept at 18℃.   ◯

9 Which of the following are high temperature methods of extending shelf life?

   A   Boiling   ◯

   B   UHT   ◯

   C   Cook-chill   ◯

   D   Pasteurisation   ◯

   E   Canning   ◯

   F   Sterilisation   ◯

   G   Baking   ◯

10 What does the E number indicate?

Designing Food Products

Lifecycle

The **lifecycle** of a food product is the time from invention to the time it's no longer made. Products are **re-invented** so that consumers will keep buying them.

Food manufacturers produce new foods in response to the **changing needs of consumers**, **environmental pressures** and **technological advances**.

The Demand for New Food Products

In the last twenty years consumers have had more money to spend on food, leading to more 'luxury' products, e.g. ice creams.

Some people are concerned about animal welfare. They want to know what products contain, e.g. free range rather than battery eggs, organic meat instead of meat from intensively reared animals.

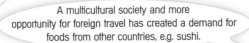

Advances in **biotechnology**, e.g. genetic engineering and cloning, are creating opportunities for new food commodities. These include vegetable oils and meats high in Omega-3 fatty acids, and plants which are resistant to drought and pests. Most hard cheese is now made using chymosin (an enzyme from GM yeast), rather than rennet. Some consumers are concerned about the use of these products.

The food industry is developing **nanotechnology**, which builds from the atom up. Nanofoods have special properties. For example, they can reduce the fat content of ice cream or mayonnaise by creating oil droplets that are full of water. Meat can have cholesterol replaced. Nutrients can be added without changing the texture or flavour of food.

Consumers are more aware of the effect of diet on health, which has led to a bigger demand for healthier options, e.g. reduced fat, low salt, high in NSP, vegan, and dairy-free food products.

Shopping trends have changed. People tend to shop less often as they can buy in bulk and store food at home, e.g. freezing, many people now buy food online, and there's an increasing awareness of the need to buy food from sustainable sources that is environmentally produced. A market has been created for food that can be frozen and/or microwaved as more people own these appliances. The increase in single households has created a demand for single portion foods, and the number of working parents and our busy lifestyles have increased the need for convenience foods.

Nutraceutical foods are considered to have medical or health benefits including the prevention and treatment of disease. Prebiotics are carbohydrates that act as food for good bacteria. They help to keep the gut healthy.

Environmental awareness has led consumers to want to reduce their carbon footprint. Concern about 'food miles' has led to an increase in farmers' markets and the use of seasonal foods. Some producers now sell locally sourced food.

As transportation improves, ingredients can be sourced globally, and there is an ever increasing variety of food available.

A multicultural society and more opportunity for foreign travel has created a demand for foods from other countries, e.g. sushi.

Designing Food

It's rare that new foods are produced. Most are **modifications** of existing products, e.g. chicken breast may be sold in cheese sauce. Using a different flavoured sauce, e.g. tomato and mushroom, creates a new dish. New products can result from a change in the shape or size of an existing one, e.g. a child-sized portion of moussaka.

Baked beans in tomato sauce are a traditional favourite. Modifications include baked beans with sausages, baked beans with meat balls, baked beans in spicy sauce, bigger baked beans, low salt baked beans, and baked beans with Omega-3. Similar new products have been produced using soya or chick peas.

Developing Products

Manufacturers identify specific **target groups** when they give a brief to a designer; e.g. 'Our sale of meat pies is beginning to slow down. How could we make them healthier and more interesting for teenagers?'

In this case the target group is teenagers. Other target groups include children, people with special dietary needs, vegans and vegetarians, and people living alone.

The **brief** gives guidelines and ideas. From this, a **design specification** can be produced. In addition, the designer may be asked to consider other factors, e.g. whether the product is environmentally friendly. When the designer has received the brief they will follow the **design process**.

The Design Process

DESIGN SPECIFICATION

- Costs under £1.50 to produce (low cost).
- Contains no animal products and is suitable for all vegetarians.
- Has to be able to be mass produced.
- Will be cook-chilled.
- Has to be savoury.
- Should contain protein from vegetables.

Research

↓

Develop design specification

↓

Generate ideas

↓

Make prototype in test kitchen

↓

Sensory evaluation and selection of final dish

↓

Modifications

↓

Develop product specification

↓

Consumer testing

↓

Final modifications

↓

Produce manufacturing specification and HACCP

↓

First factory production run

↓

Trialling (test marketing)

↓

Final modifications

↓

Product launch

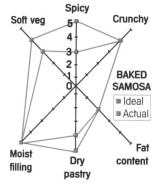

Radar Graph / Star Profile

BAKED SAMOSA
- Ideal
- Actual

Spicy, Crunchy, Fat content, Dry pastry, Moist filling, Soft veg

Specifications

Types of Specification

There are three different types of specification that you need to understand:

- The **design specification** is used during the design stage, and produced by the manufacturer and designer.
- The **product specification** is used to show others what the product should be like. Food products are often designed in one part of the country, but made across the UK. It's important that the specification has sufficient detail to help everyone understand what the final product must be like.
- The **manufacturing specification** is used to make sure that all products are identical and safe.

Design Specification

The **design specification** is a guideline for designers. It's developed from the initial brief, and describes what the product, not yet designed, is intending to do.

The designer and manufacturer work together to develop the design specification. Designers write down the design specification, and use it to make sure that any ideas they develop meet the needs of the **manufacturer** and **consumer**.

Design specifications should include the following details about a product:

- a description of the organoleptic properties
- purpose and function
- cost
- nutritional requirements
- particular ingredients to be used, e.g. ready made sauce
- the type of storage, e.g. chill cabinet
- environmental issues, e.g. packaging
- information about manufacturing, e.g. suitability for mass production.

If the brief is to produce a healthy savoury product that can be put into children's packed lunches, the design specification might look like the example below.

Design Specification

Healthy savoury product for children's packed lunch:
- costs under 60p to produce
- suitable for children
- suitable for mass production
- has to be savoury
- can be sold as a healthy option
- should be high in protein
- can be packaged as an individual portion
- suitable for sale in supermarkets.

Product Specification

The product specification is developed once the final dish has been designed.

The **product specification**...
- explains what the product should be like
- often includes a photograph
- describes colour, texture, flavour
- gives measurements and tolerance for sizes and volume
- includes details of packaging and storage
- provides details about shelf life
- includes the nutritional profile
- identifies potential allergy risks.

Product Specification

22–24cm diameter

45–50g tomato passata

weighs between 150–170g when cooked

30–35g grated Cheddar cheese over tomato topping

Olives

Green peppers

2–2.5cm deep

Pizza bread base

Manufacturing Specification

The **manufacturing specification** is usually top secret. It's a technical specification used throughout manufacture to ensure every product is identical. It forms part of the **quality assurance system**. The manufacturing specification describes everything that's needed in making the product, including how it should be **prepared**, **packaged** and **stored**.

The manufacturing specification includes...
- the recipe
- food hygiene procedures
- the sizes of the dish, including tolerances

- details of ingredients, which are very specific, e.g. chicken breast rather than chicken
- detailed instructions for preparing ingredients, e.g. length of time for mixing or kneading
- which supplier ingredients will come from
- details of standard components, including the supplier
- cost of ingredients and recommended retail price (RRP)
- portion control
- how it will be packaged
- shelf life of the finished product.

Quick Test

1. What word describes the time from which a food product is invented until it's no longer made?
2. When is the product specification developed?
3. The manufacturing specification is usually top secret. **True** or **false**?
4. In which specification would detailed hygiene procedures be found?

KEY WORDS
Make sure you understand these words before moving on!
- Lifecycle
- Target groups
- Brief
- Design specification
- Product specification
- Manufacturing specification

Specifications

Portion Control

Portion control ensures that all the products are **identical**. The size and shapes of containers, formers and cutters need to be written into the specification for this to happen. If too large a cutter is used in the production of digestive biscuits, it causes problems when the biscuits are wrapped, as the wrapper is made to fit a specific size of biscuit.

Industrial Roller Used to Cut Biscuits

Standard Components

During the design stage, manufacturers may decide that they want to use a **standard component**.

Standard components are **ready made products** (pre-manufactured), for example…

- frozen / chilled pastry / pastry mix
- decorations, e.g. icing, edible decorations
- pizza bases / pastry cases
- spice blends
- ready made fillings / sauces / cake and bread mixes
- stock cubes, gravy mix and powdered soup.

Standard Components include Spice Blends such as Curry Powder

Advantages of Using Standard Components

- Components can be bought in bulk
- Ensures consistency of flavour, texture, colour, shape, size, weight, depth and outcome enabling an exact replication of each product
- Saves time in manufacturing process
- Less effort in manufacturing process
- Specific requirements of companies can be met, ensuring exact specifications can be maintained
- Exact costs can be worked out
- Less equipment needed
- Allows work within designated tolerances
- A less-skilled workforce required
- Less risk of cross contamination, e.g. a sandwich manufacturer buying cooked chicken instead of cooking raw chicken

Disadvantages of Using Standard Components

- Time needed for ordering and delivery
- There may be supply problems
- Can be more expensive
- They may have poor sensory qualities
- Other food companies may use the same components

Researching

Designers need to conduct different types of research before they develop new foods.

This can involve two types of research:

1. **primary research** – collecting your own original information, which didn't exist before
2. **secondary research** – information already collected by someone else.

Primary	Research	Secondary
• Interviews – face to face / telephone / online • Questionnaires / surveys • Focus groups • Consumer panels • Disassembling products		• Books • Magazine or newspaper articles • Leaflets • Information from organisations, e.g. Vegetarian Society

Disassembly

Disassembly means taking things apart. It's used by designers to develop their ideas.

We can work out how dishes are made by taking them apart. In some cases, like sausage rolls or samosas, individual components can be weighed. In other products, the ingredients are changed by cooking. If this is the case, the designers need to work out the function of the ingredients.

By looking at the information on the packet, we can see how much the **product costs**, and how many items are in the packet. From this we can work out the **cost per item**.

The packet also provides **nutritional information**. This information can help the designers create a healthier version of the product. The information on the packet about storage, shelf life and reheating methods may also be used to design a new product.

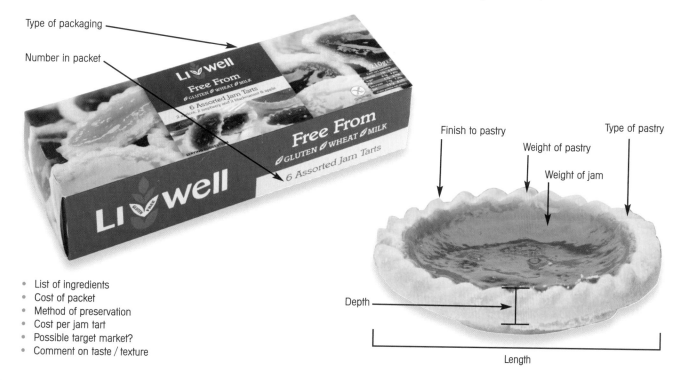

Type of packaging

Number in packet

- List of ingredients
- Cost of packet
- Method of preservation
- Cost per jam tart
- Possible target market?
- Comment on taste / texture

Finish to pastry

Weight of pastry

Weight of jam

Type of pastry

Depth

Length

Computers: Research and Design

Research Using Computers

Computers are an excellent research tool for finding out and recording information.

Computers can be used to...

- write out a questionnaire or survey, and **analyse** the information using a database
- **record the results** of observations, questionnaires, surveys and interviews with a word processing program
- record results using a **spreadsheet**
- **speed up communication** with individuals or organisations by the use of e-mail
- **interview** people using video conferencing.

Another form of electronic media used in research is **EPOS** (electronic point of sale systems). As food passes through the till in supermarkets, a database is built, which informs how well a particular product is selling. Other forms of electronic media are TV, DVD, CD and software programs.

Scaling up Samosa Recipe Using Spreadsheet

Portions	10	100	1000
Filo Pastry	0.72	7.2	72
Potato	0.5	5	50
Carrot	0.2	2	20
Peas	0.6	6	60
Onion	0.1	1	10
Chilli	0.6	6	60
Coriander	0.1	1	10
Pepper	0.1	1	10
Salt	0.1	1	10
	3.02	30.2	302
Discount	0%	12%	20%
	3.02	26.576	241.6
Price/samosa	£0.302	£0.26576	£0.2416

The Internet

The **internet** is used to find out how popular existing products are. You can look at competitors' products via their websites. These products can then be disassembled to work out ingredients, nutritional profile costs, weight and size.

The internet is also used to find out...

- about product ideas and new recipes
- where to source ingredients
- new information about packaging and storage
- how products are being advertised online, as well as in newspapers, magazines, TV, radio and cinema.

Why Use Computer Aided Design?

There are lots of reasons for using **Computer Aided Design** (CAD).

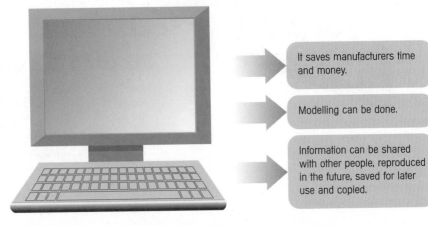

Mathematical work is done speedily and accurately, which avoids human error.

Work is produced quickly, efficiently, neatly and accurately.

It's easy to make changes.

It saves manufacturers time and money.

Modelling can be done.

Information can be shared with other people, reproduced in the future, saved for later use and copied.

Modelling

Modelling is the representation of a real object on the computer screen. Ideas can be modelled without having to actually make anything. Modelling is used to predict what happens when numbers change, i.e. in a recipe or cost. It shows the effect of different ingredients on the structure and nutritional profile of a product. The effect of micro-organisms can be modelled by very specialised programs to show, for example, how bacteria would grow in different conditions, e.g. chilled, frozen, ambient.

Computers and Design

CAD can be used for the following:
- research – both primary and secondary
- HACCP charts
- producing flow charts
- nutritional analysis
- modelling costs
- drawing virtual dishes
- modelling changes to recipes
- labels designed with graphic programs
- risk assessment
- scaling up recipes using spreadsheets
- modelling growth of bacteria
- sensory evaluations
- designing packaging.

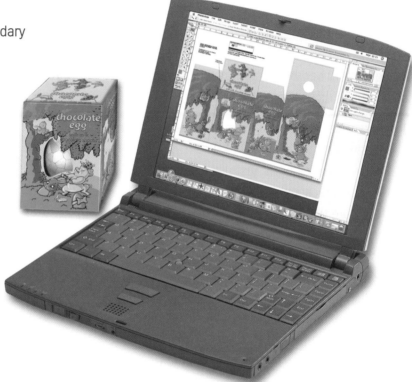

Quick Test

1. Why is portion control used?
2. Do questionnaires provide secondary or primary research information?
3. Using computers speeds up communications. **True** or **false**?
4. What would be used to scale up a recipe?
5. A virtual dish only exists on the computer, not in real life. **True** or **false**?

Equipment

Equipment

Hand-held tools may be used in the home to reduce the size of food by grating, chopping, slicing, pulping, dicing, milling, grinding and shredding.

Designers make **prototypes** in the test kitchen. They use small electrical equipment to...

* obtain **consistent results**
* guarantee the **quality of the outcome**
* **avoid human error**.

Manufacturers use large scale equipment for the same reasons, and also because it saves time, labour and money.

Safety

All equipment can be dangerous if not used, cleaned and stored correctly.

To **prevent accidents and injuries** in the home and in industry...

* follow manufacturers' instructions carefully
* avoid distractions
* take care with hot liquids, e.g. fit lids securely on blenders
* use heat resistant gloves or handles where necessary
* switch off gas if a leak is suspected
* don't have open windows near naked flames
* plugs must be correctly wired and fused
* flexes mustn't be frayed or allowed to trail
* equipment should have passed PAT tests and be regularly checked and maintained
* some workers may need to use chain mail gloves, rubber gloves or sleeve protectors
* masks and eye protection may be needed.

In the food industry, part of the **HACCP procedure** is to **train workers**. No one is allowed to operate machinery until they have been trained how to do so correctly and safely. Industrial machines must be fitted with safety switches and guards, and have emergency stop buttons.

Many accidents in the home are caused by the incorrect use of sharp knives. Any cutting or chopping should be done in the correct way:

1. Use the correct sharp knife for the task.
2. Hold a knife by the handle and use point down when cutting.
3. Keep your fingers away from the blade by holding food with clawed fingers or in a 'bridge'.
4. Don't have greasy hands.
5. Cut on a stable surface.

Bridge

Equipment in Test Kitchens

Home economists in test kitchens use similar equipment to what you use at home and school. Knives are used for cutting and chopping and wooden spoons for mixing. Sometimes home economists use **electrical appliances** like processors or mixers, so they can make sure **mixtures are always mixed for the same time** at **the same speed**. This is important when they are comparing different samples. **Electric scales** are used because they're **very accurate** and can **measure very small quantities**.

Computer Integrated Manufacture (CIM) Edexcel • OCR

In large scale manufacturing food products may be made using **Computer Integrated Manufacture** (**CIM**). The **entire process** is **controlled by computers**.

Ingredients are stored in large vats or silos and pumped through pipes when they're needed. The speed of the flow is controlled by a computer. A valve is opened by the computer to allow the ingredients to flow out into a container attached to a load cell. Once the weight is reached the valve is closed by the computer.

Mixing takes place in enclosed containers. The speed of – and time taken for – mixing is controlled by a computer.

For products like biscuits, the mixture is…
* emptied onto a conveyor belt
* rolled to the correct thickness by large rollers
* cut out by shaped rollers.

The biscuits continue on the conveyor belt to a computer-controlled tunnel oven, then to a cooling chamber and the packaging area. **Throughout production** the **biscuits aren't touched by a person**.

Ingredients Stored in Large Silos

Quick Test

1. Why do designers use small electrical equipment?
2. Apart from time and labour, what else do manufacturers save by using electrical equipment?
3. It's important to follow manufacturers' instructions. **True** or **false**?
4. Workers using machinery must be trained as part of which procedure?
5. What three things must industrial machines be fitted with?

KEY WORDS
Make sure you understand these words before moving on!
* Guards
* Emergency stop buttons
* Computer Integrated Manufacture (CIM)

Sensory Analysis

The Five Senses

Sensory analysis involves using our five senses to evaluate whether or not we like a dish.

We use all of our five **senses** when we eat to give us information about food.

Sensory analysis is used to…

* gather information about the product
* discover what consumers prefer
* compare food with other existing products
* evaluate the sensory characteristics of a product
* identify where improvements are needed
* improve future products
* produce a product that will sell.

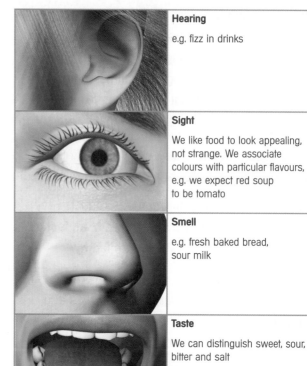

Hearing	e.g. fizz in drinks
Sight	We like food to look appealing, not strange. We associate colours with particular flavours, e.g. we expect red soup to be tomato
Smell	e.g. fresh baked bread, sour milk
Taste	We can distinguish sweet, sour, bitter and salt
Touch	Hands – ripeness of fruit or vegetables Mouth – texture or feeling in mouth, e.g. exploding candy or soggy biscuits

Conducting Sensory Analysis

To ensure a **fair test**, sensory analysis should take place in **controlled conditions**:

* A quiet area to avoid disturbance.
* An area where there's no smell of other foods.
* An area where the light can be changed.
* Somewhere that has individual booths.
* Small quantities of food served on identical sized and coloured dishes.
* Codes used for products to prevent testers being influenced (blind testing).
* Clear instructions given to testers.
* Charts available to complete.
* Water or a cracker to clear the palate.

Using Sensory Analysis

Sensory analysis is used at different stages of product development. Initially, **focus** (discussion) **groups** can be used to discuss products that are already on the market, to see what consumers would like to buy.

Some sensory analysis testing needs to be done as part of **evaluating new dishes** that are being developed. The testing can be done by trained testers or by members of the public. It can take place in special sensory analysis booths, in public places and private homes.

Techniques for Testing

Preference testing is used to find out which product people **like best**. The two different kinds of preference testing are…

1 **hedonic rating** tests
2 **paired preference** tests.

In **hedonic rating** tests, testers indicate their opinion of one or more samples of food, using an uneven numbered scale, where 1 is 'dislike a lot' and 5 is 'like a lot'. The food is ranked using the total scores.

In **paired preference** tests, testers are given two similar samples of food and they have to indicate which sample they prefer, e.g. Sample A (tuna fishcakes) or Sample B (salmon fishcakes).

Smiley faces may be used when testing food with young children so they understand what to do. The test is usually done with the help of an adult.

Results of Testing with Young Children

Sample	
34712	😊
79655	🙁
29731	😐
49623	😊

Paired Preference Tests

Please indicate which sample you prefer.

Smiley Faces

Like a lot   Like a little   Neither like nor dislike   Dislike a little   Dislike a lot

Quick Test

1 Sensory analysis is used at different stages in the design process. **True** or **false**?
2 Using a code for dishes prevents testers being influenced. What is the name of this kind of testing?
3 Why is hedonic rating used?
4 What could you use in place of numbers when testing food with children?

KEY WORDS

Make sure you understand these words before moving on!
- Sensory analysis
- Senses
- Fair test
- Focus groups
- Hedonic rating
- Paired preference

Sensory Analysis

Discriminatory Testing

Discriminatory tests (difference tests) are used to see if people can tell the difference between two very **similar samples**, e.g. when an ingredient or quantity of an ingredient is changed, or when manufacturers are copying another brand, e.g. two brands of cheese and onion crisps.

Two different kinds of test can be used:
1. **triangle testing**
2. **A not A testing**.

In **triangle testing** three samples are tested. Two samples are the same, one is different. The tester has to identify the 'odd one out'. For example, when beans in tomato sauce have the salt content reduced, this test can be used to see if consumers can tell the difference.

In **A not A testing**, testers are given a control sample to try. They are then given two further samples. One of these is like the control (A) sample and one is different (not A). They're asked to identify which one is like the control sample (A).

Triangle Testing

Which one is the odd one out?

A not A Testing

Which one is the same?

A

Attribute Testing

Attribute testing (star profile) is used...
- as part of the disassembly of other dishes
- to show what the finished product should be like (ideal profile)
- to build up a detailed evaluation to compare against the ideal
- to show if modifications are needed.

The attributes (characteristics) to be tested are drawn on the leg of a **radar graph**. The legs are divided into 5 equal sections and testers are asked to indicate how strong each attribute is (5 = very strong, 1 = very weak).

Radar Graph / Star Profile

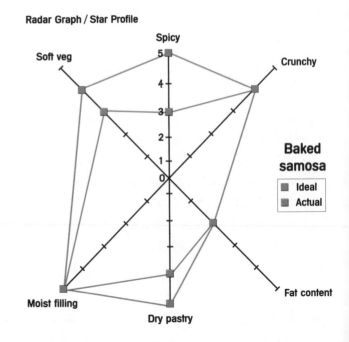

Baked samosa
- Ideal
- Actual

Facts About Flow Charts

Once a new product is designed, a **flow chart** is developed. Flow charts show complex systems in a simple diagram. They're all written using the **standard BSI symbols** below.

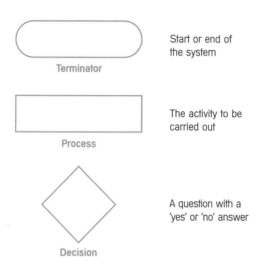

Terminator — Start or end of the system

Process — The activity to be carried out

Decision — A question with a 'yes' or 'no' answer

If the feedback from the question is 'yes' the process moves forward. If it's 'no' the process returns to the previous stage.

Used to show the flow of work

Designers work from flow charts to make sure that every time they make the product it's the same (identical). A flow chart also allows the food manufacturer to set up a production line, which will result in a good quality, safe final product.

Here is an example of a flow chart.

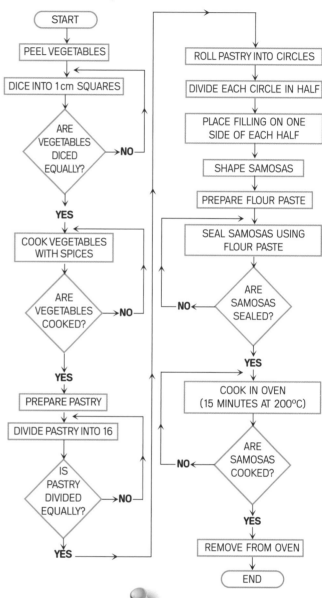

Quick Test

1. Why is discriminatory testing used?
2. In triangle testing, how many samples are the same?
3. What is another name for attribute testing?
4. A flow chart is a diagram. **True** or **false**?
5. What does the terminator symbol show?
6. What does this symbol indicate?

KEY WORDS

Make sure you understand these words before moving on!
- Triangle testing
- A not A testing
- Attribute testing
- Flow chart
- Terminator
- Process
- Decision

Practice Questions

1 Which of these sentences refer to a design specification? Tick the correct options.

A A design specification provides details about shelf life. ☐

B A design specification details packaging. ☐

C A design specification describes what the product is intended to do. ☐

D Designers write a design specification down, and use it to make sure any ideas they develop meet the needs of the consumers and manufacturer. ☐

E A design specification includes a recipe. ☐

F A design specification often includes photographs. ☐

G A design specification is a guideline for designers. ☐

H A design specification describes colour, texture and flavour. ☐

2 Fill in the missing words to complete the following sentences.

_____ _____ ensures that all products are identical. The size

and _____ of containers needs to be _____ into the specification.

3 Which of the following is a disadvantage of using standard components? Tick the correct option.

A Less equipment needed ☐   **B** Ensures a consistency of flavour ☐

C Saves time ☐   **D** There may be supply problems ☐

4 Explain the difference between primary and secondary research.

_____

_____

_____

5 Which of the following are methods used in primary research? Tick the correct options.

A Newspaper articles ☐   **B** Interviews ☐

C Consumer panels ☐   **D** Books ☐

E Leaflets ☐   **F** Focus groups ☐

G Disassembling products ☐   **H** Questionnaires ☐

6 How does CAD help with mathematical work?

_____

7 In what way can the internet be useful when researching existing food products? Tick the correct option.

    A   The internet can tell you about the manufacturing specification of an existing product. ⬭

    B   The internet can tell you how popular existing products are. ⬭

    C   The internet can tell you what HACCP procedures are used in existing products. ⬭

    D   The internet can tell you the recipe of an existing product. ⬭

8 Which of the following statements are true? Tick the correct options.

    A   Using CAD, the effect of bacteria on a product can be modelled. ⬭

    B   Recipes can be scaled up quickly and accurately. ⬭

    C   It's difficult to make changes when using CAD. ⬭

    D   Using CAD means that any work can't be saved. ⬭

    E   Using CAD makes it easy for designers to share their work with other people. ⬭

9 Fill in the missing words to name the sensory analysis tests.

In _____, testers are given a control sample to try, then

given two further samples, one of which is the same as the control. In _____

_____, attributes are drawn on the legs of a radar graph. In _____

_____, three samples are tested: two are the same, one is different. In

_____ _____, testers are given two

similar samples and are asked to indicate their preference. In _____

_____, testers indicate their preference of food samples using an unevenly numbered scale.

10 Draw the symbols for process, decision and terminator, which are used in a flow chart.

Process   **Decision**   **Terminator**

Scales of Production

Scales of Production

Manufacturers decide the **scale of production** depending on the number of products predicted to be sold and the shelf life.

Just in Time means that materials are delivered to the manufacturer just in time for them to make products for immediate dispatch to retailers. This means products don't need to be stored in a factory. This cuts down waste and reduces risk of bacterial contamination.

One-Off Production

One-off production is also known as jobbing. One-off products...
- include cakes for special occasions
- include prototypes produced in a test kitchen
- are used by small scale manufacturers
- can be costly to produce
- rely on skilled workers
- don't require very specialised equipment.

Mass Production

Mass production means making many **identical products**.

Small scale manufacturers use batch production to make a variety of products.

In batch production...
- large quantities of a product can be made efficiently
- there are short runs of identical products
- production is completed by one person or by a team
- equipment can be adapted for use
- skilled workers are needed
- products can be made in a test kitchen
- recipes can be modified easily.

Continuous flow makes products with a long shelf-life in large quantities, e.g. crisps and chocolate.

Continuous flow...
- requires very specialised machinery
- products are made 24 hours a day, 7 days a week
- machinery can only be used to make one product
- often relies on Computer Aided Manufacture (CAM) or Computer Integrated Manufacture (CIM)
- needs semi-skilled or unskilled labour.

Batch Production

Continuous Flow

Computer Aided Manufacture

Why Use CAM?

Computer Aided Manufacture (CAM) is incorporated into continuous flow production lines. Computers do the work of semi-skilled and unskilled workers. Highly skilled computer technicians are required.

Food manufacturers use computers in many stages of production because they…
- can run all day, every day, without tea breaks
- save on labour costs
- remove human error
- assess thousands of products in minutes
- detect things that the human eye cannot see
- increase productivity
- are more hygienic and reliable, as the food isn't touched.

How CAM is Used in Industry

In Computer Aided Manufacture, computers can be used for many processes. Some examples are given below.

Control	Use
Load cells	Measure weight and volume, e.g. ingredients in the recipe or in the finished product
Light refractor	Detects colour change, e.g. baked goods which are over or under cooked, the green of vegetables, and any dirt or stones that may be mixed in
Light detector	Used to control the viscosity (thickness) of sauces
Metal detector	Detects metal throughout the manufacturing and packaging process
Temperature sensor	Sensors are set to maintain temperatures within a given tolerance, e.g. in cooking, cooling, chilling and freezing; temperature of chocolate for enrobing
Electronic eye	Counts the number of products
Moisture sensor	Ensures that baked products are crispy by measuring water content, e.g. biscuits
pH sensor	Tests the acidity level, e.g. pickles and chutneys
Micro-biological sensor	Detects the presence of bacteria

When the control detects a problem, appropriate remedial action is taken. This may include an **automatic adjustment** being made by the computer, e.g. oven temperatures. In other cases it could be an alarm sounding, a light flashing, or the food may be blown or pushed off the production line.

Quality Assurance and Quality Control

Quality

Consumers expect food to be **safe to eat**, to always **look and taste the same**, and be the **same size**. If the food is reliable you're more likely to buy it again. In the food industry, quality assurance and quality control processes are used to make sure that products meet our expectations.

Manufacturers have to know what their customers want, so they can design foods to meet these needs.

You might want a pizza to…
- be inexpensive
- have a large amount of ham
- look just like a real Italian pizza.

If the pizza meets your needs you'll think it is good 'quality'.

Quality Assurance

Quality assurance is a **guarantee of quality**. Manufacturers assure their customers that a product will be of a **consistent quality** (the same every time it is bought).

Companies who reach **high standards** for delivering quality products and services can gain an **ISO9000 certificate**.

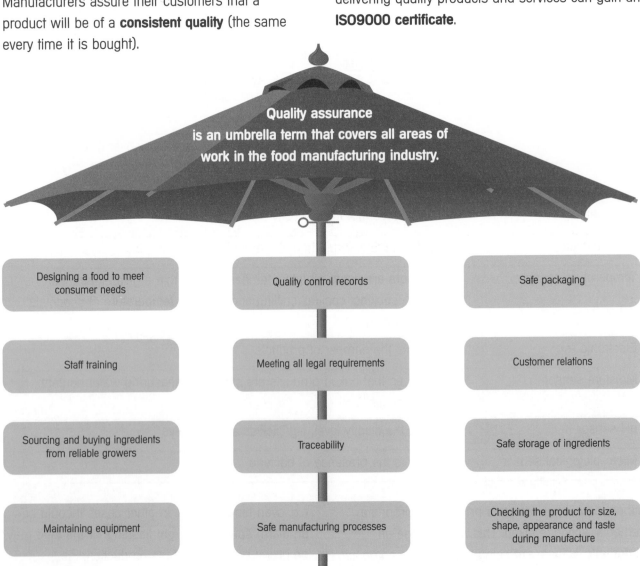

Quality assurance is an umbrella term that covers all areas of work in the food manufacturing industry.

Designing a food to meet consumer needs

Quality control records

Safe packaging

Staff training

Meeting all legal requirements

Customer relations

Sourcing and buying ingredients from reliable growers

Traceability

Safe storage of ingredients

Maintaining equipment

Safe manufacturing processes

Checking the product for size, shape, appearance and taste during manufacture

Quality Assurance and Quality Control

Quality Control

Quality control is one part of the quality assurance process. It involves checking the quality of the product at three stages:

- **during design**
- **during manufacture**
- **at the end of manufacture**.

All manufacturing industries use quality control to make sure the products they're making are of an acceptable standard.

In the food industry quality control is even more important. Manufacturers identify stages in production where these checks must be made. They are called Critical Control Points (CCP) and Quality Control Points (QCP).

CCPs check the **safety** of food to make sure it doesn't cause illness when it's eaten. These CCPs are identified as part of the Hazard Analysis and Critical Control Point (HACCP) procedure. If manufacturers make people ill, then they will be investigated by an Environmental Health officer, and could face closure of their business, large fines, or even prison.

QCPs are checks undertaken during manufacture. Food is inspected to ensure that the size and shape, appearance, taste and texture meet the product specification. If it fails to meet these standards it will affect the overall quality of the final product. The product may have to be sold as a 'second', e.g. poorly enrobed biscuits, or thrown away.

In both cases, manufacturers could lose money, so they want to make sure that they meet these quality standards.

The 1990 Food Safety Act   Edexcel • OCR

The 1990 Food Safety Act makes food manufacturers legally responsible for making sure that the food they make and sell is safe to eat. It's enforced by Environmental Health officers and Trading Standards officers.

Environmental Health officers make sure that food is produced, manufactured, stored and presented for sale without causing risk to consumers. They test samples of food and condemn unsafe food. They inspect food at ports, slaughter houses and food premises. They also investigate cases of food poisoning, run food hygiene courses, give advice and suggest improvements.

Trading Standards officers check the quality of food, so no misleading claims are made. They check that labels are accurate and ingredients are safe to use. They also check weighing and measuring equipment in shops and factories, and give advice to consumers.

Quick Test

1. Where is a prototype made?
2. What does CAM stand for?
3. What does quality assurance guarantee?
4. Quality control is a part of which process?
5. Quality control points check that food is safe to eat. **True** or **false**?
6. Which officer is responsible for checking that labels are accurate?

KEY WORDS

Make sure you understand these words before moving on!

- Jobbing
- Mass production
- Batch production
- Continuous flow
- Computer Aided Manufacture
- Quality assurance
- Quality control
- Environmental Health officers
- Trading Standards officers

HACCP

Hazards

A hazard is anything that may **go wrong** and **cause harm** to someone. When a new product is being designed a hazard analysis must be carried out. This means working out what could go wrong during manufacture in order to plan how to stop it happening. The system used in food manufacturing is Hazard Analysis and Critical Control Points, or **HACCP**.

Types of Hazard

There are three types of hazard in food production:

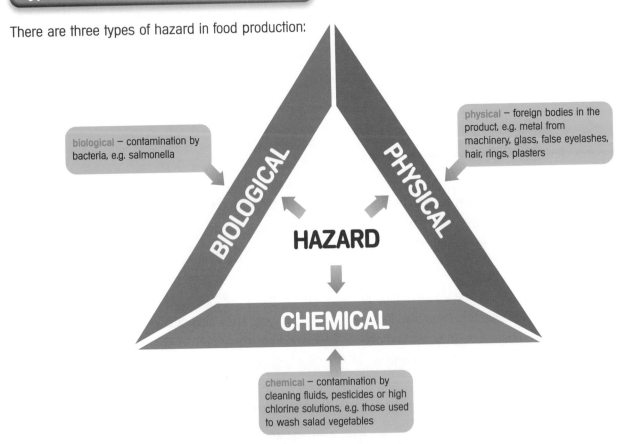

biological – contamination by bacteria, e.g. salmonella

physical – foreign bodies in the product, e.g. metal from machinery, glass, false eyelashes, hair, rings, plasters

chemical – contamination by cleaning fluids, pesticides or high chlorine solutions, e.g. those used to wash salad vegetables

They must all be **monitored** and **controlled** by the manufacturer.

Hazards can occur at any stage in food production:
- growing and harvesting raw ingredients
- processing ingredients, such as milling wheat
- during transportation of ingredients
- storage of ingredients
- preparation of ingredients
- cooking
- cooling
- storage of the products by the manufacturer
- transportation to – and storage by – the retailer
- transport, storage and reheating by the consumer (most food poisoning happens because the consumer doesn't follow the storage and reheating instructions given by the manufacturer).

HACCP Charts

To produce a HACCP chart you should do the following:

- List the manufacturing processes.
- Identify where risks may happen.
- Decide which are critical to the safety of the consumer – are these high or low risk?
- Set tolerances for the controls.

- Plan how the risks may be removed or reduced to an acceptable standard or level.
- Plan how controls will be monitored or checked.
- Decide what will be done if there is a problem (**remedial action**).

Below is a **section** of a HACCP chart for a pizza.

CCP/ QCP	Process	Hazard	Risk Assessment	Control	Test	Remedial Action
CCP	Delivery of ingredients	Dirty van	High	Check container	Visual	Refuse delivery Find reliable supplier
CCP	Delivery of mozzarella	Mozzarella contains listeria	High	Random sample tested	Microbiological	Discard and inform Environmental Health officer
CCP	Delivery of meat	Meat too warm	High	Test temperature	Use temperature probe 1–4°C	Refuse delivery Find reliable supplier
CCP	Collect ingredients	Open bags	High	Check bags	Visual	Discard
CCP	Collecting /weighing ingredients	Food out of date	High	Check dates Use **First In First Out** (FIFO) stock rotation	Visual	Discard
CCP	Weigh ingredients	Dirty workers	High	Check workforce trained	Basic Food Hygiene Cert.	Retrain workers
QCP	Mix dough	Dough insufficiently mixed	Low	Mix 5 minutes	Visual	Mix 2 minutes longer

Quick Test

1. What is a hazard?
2. What does HACCP stand for?
3. What does FIFO stand for?
4. There are two main hazards in food production – physical and chemical. **True** or **false**?
5. What is the last stage in a HACCP chart?

KEY WORDS
Make sure you understand these words before moving on!
- Hazard Analysis and Critical Control Points
- Biological
- Physical
- Chemical
- Remedial action

Food Labelling

Labelling

Labelling is controlled by **European Union** (EU) regulations.

Some information on packaging is a **legal requirement** (it has to be included by law). Labels must be in a language that can be understood in the country of use. Information on labels must inform the consumer and be accurate.

Trading Standards officers make sure that labels don't describe food in a false or misleading way. If they do, manufacturers can be prosecuted.

Legal Requirements on Labels

The **name** identifies the food. Processed foods must also be identified by the cooking method, e.g. smoked, roast.

Contains GM soya or maize allows consumers to make an ethical choice.

Weight / volume:
'e' indicates approximate weight – allows for tolerances.

Ingredients are listed in **descending order of weight**. The largest amount is first on the list and the smallest amount is the last.

Contains nuts or **may contain traces of nuts** indicates whether the product may have been in contact with nuts during manufacture.

Manufacturer's name or address allows consumers to contact the manufacturer.

Country of origin.

Shelf life details: the best before date indicates that food is safe to eat but the quality will begin to deteriorate. After the use by date there is a risk of food poisoning. The display by / sell by date tells the retailer what to do with the product.

Instructions for use / heating instructions ensure that the product is cooked at the right temperature and that it's safe to eat.

Storage instructions are shown in words, symbols or temperatures.

GREENFIELD'S BAKED BEANS IN TOMATO SAUCE

contains GM Soya

e210g

NUTRITIONAL INFORMATION

Typical Values	Per 100g	Per Serving (207g)
Energy	279 kJ/	577 kJ/
	66 kcal	136 kcal
Protein	4.7g	9.7g
Carbohydrate	11.3g	23.3g
(of which sugars)	3.4g	7.1g
Fat	0.2g	0.4g
(of which saturated)	Trace	Trace
Fibre	3.7g	7.7g
Sodium	0.3g	0.7g

Per Serving (207g):
136 calories   0.4g fat

INGREDIENTS

Beans (50%), Tomatoes (25%), Water, Sugar, Modified cornflour, Salt, Vinegar, Sweeteners: acesulfame, potassium, spice extracts, herb extracts. FREE FROM ARTIFICIAL FLAVOURS, COLOURS AND PRESERVATIVES. Warning. May contain nuts.

TO OPEN CAN

Place on a flat surface and lift tab fully. Turn can and peel back lid. Gently ease lid off.

GUARANTEE

If you are not entirely satisfied with this product write to us quoting the batch code on the base of the can. Your statutory rights are not affected.

GREENFIELDS FOODS CO LTD
OLDHAM
LANCS
OL6 6WX U.K.

BEST BEFORE END AND BATCH CODE
SEE BASE OF CAN.

HEATING INSTRUCTIONS

Empty contents into a saucepan and stir gently whilst heating. Do not boil.

(650W) Empty contents into a suitable container. Cover and heat on full power for 2 minutes. Stir and heat for a further 2 minutes.

Put any unused contents into a covered container and use within 2 days.

5 0057 024909

Voluntary Information on Labels

The **voluntary information** on labels includes...

- a detailed description, e.g. beans **in tomato sauce**
- cost
- an illustration – this mustn't be misleading
- environmental issues, e.g. dolphin friendly
- a bar code, which isn't legally required but needed by most retailers
- a batch / lot mark, which allows the food to be traced back to when and where it was produced if there's a problem
- nutritional information

- serving suggestions
- special claims, like '**low fat**'. These terms have a legal definition. They don't mean that a product is healthy, as low fat products are often high in sugar or salt.

Food products use terms such as farm fresh, traditional, country fresh and wholesome, which don't have a clear meaning. These terms are used to **market** the food. Manufacturers don't have to label foods as suitable for vegetarians, but it's a selling point.

Environmental Symbols

	SPI System (PET numbers from 1–7 indicate type of plastic).	Mobius loop shows that packaging is recyclable. The number inside or below the loop indicates the percentage of recycled materials used.	Glass can be recycled and should be put in a bottle bank.
	Recyclable aluminium.		
	Recyclable steel.		Do not litter.

Quick Test

1. What is meant by a legal requirement?
2. Does the information on a label have to be accurate by law?
3. Nutritional information is a legal requirement. **True** or **false**?
4. On a label what could be shown instead of the weight?
5. Do manufacturers have to label foods as suitable for a vegetarian?

KEY WORDS
Make sure you understand these words before moving on!
- Legal requirement
- Voluntary information

Packaging

Functions of Packaging

There are concerns about the environment, so manufacturers are trying to use **minimal amounts** of packaging. Some packaging is essential because it has important functions to perform.

Packaging...
- **protects** from physical damage and prevents tampering
- **preserves** and extends shelf life
- **contains** during transportation and when displayed
- **identifies** the product
- **attracts** consumers
- **advertises** and **informs**.

Products have different levels of packaging, which makes handling, storage, transportation and displaying easier:
- **Primary packaging** contains the food product.
- **Secondary packaging** holds several products together.
- **Transit packaging** is used when products are being transported to the point of sale.

The packaging industry is developing **nanotechnology** to create labels that **change colour** if food is spoiled. This means that some packaging will be able to detect if it has been tampered with, and alert the customer.

Primary Packaging

Packet

Secondary Packaging

Packets in a Box

Transit Packaging

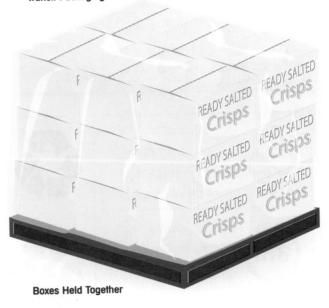

Boxes Held Together

Card and Paperboard

The **advantages** of using card and **paperboard** are that they...
- are easily printed on
- are strong
- are lightweight
- are produced in different thicknesses
- are cheap
- are biodegradable
- can be recycled
- protect and insulate if they're corrugated
- can be easily folded into different shapes.

The main **disadvantage** of card and paper is that it isn't water resistant, unless waxed.

Glass

The **advantages** of using **glass** are that it's transparent so consumers can see the product, it can be filled with hot product (heat resistant), it's rigid, and it can be recycled and reused.

The main **disadvantage** of using glass is that it's breakable and heavy, so can be expensive to transport.

Packaging

Metal

The main **advantages** of using **metal** are that it...

- is easy to open (ring pulls)
- is recyclable (aluminium)
- extends shelf life (canning).

Foil also has several **advantages**. Foil containers can be used to heat foods in an oven, foil has different thicknesses, and aluminium foil can be used to laminate paper, to protect and improve the appearance of packaging.

The **disadvantage** of using metal is that it reacts with some food, so some cans must be lined.

Plastics

Different types of **plastic** have individual characteristics. For example, some plastics are recyclable and heat resistant.

The main **advantages** of using plastic are that it's lightweight, durable, flexible or rigid, cheap to produce, easily printed on, resistant to acids / chemicals, and it's water resistant. Plastic also cushions and protects foods.

Plastics Used for Packaging

Four main plastics are used for packaging:

1. **PP (polypropylene)** prevents food drying out, and can withstand high temperatures in microwave ovens, so is used for frozen and cook-chill ready-prepared meals. Examples of polypropylene are clingfilm, yoghurt containers and bottle caps.
2. **PET (polyester)** can be used as a film, and is used in drinks. Examples of PET are carbonated drinks bottles, and microwavable packaging, film and containers.
3. **PVC (polyvinylchloride)** is resistant to acids, resistant to chemicals, can withstand high temperatures, and is flexible.
4. **PS (expanded polystyrene)** protects food (it has a cushioning effect), has good heat insulation properties, and can be brittle. An example of expanded polystyrene is the clam shells used for take away foods, hot drinks and meat trays.

Quick Test

1. Packaging contains food during transport. **True** or **false**?
2. Why is paperboard waxed?
3. Why are ring pulls used on metal cans?
4. Plastic can be flexible or rigid. **True** or **false**?
5. Which type of plastic is brittle?

KEY WORDS

Make sure you understand these words before moving on!

- Primary packaging
- Secondary packaging
- Transit packaging
- Paperboard
- Glass
- Metal
- Foil
- Plastic

Practice Questions

1 Which of the following are legal requirements for labelling? Tick the correct options.

A Name of food ⬡

B Cost ⬡

C Nutritional information ⬡

D Country of origin ⬡

E Weight / volume ⬡

F Special claims ⬡

G Ingredients ⬡

H Bar code ⬡

2 Fill in the missing words to complete the following table.

Type of Hazard	Example of Contamination
a)	Cleaning fluids, pesticide, chlorine solutions
Biological	**b)**
c)	Hair, metal, jewellery

3 Circle the correct options in the following sentences.

a) Paperboard is **cheap** / **rigid**.

b) Glass is **lightweight** / **breakable**.

c) Metal is **recyclable** / **biodegradable**.

d) Plastics are **lightweight** / **not water resistant.**

e) Polypropylene is used to make **clamshell** / **yoghurt containers**.

f) PET is used to package **hot drinks** / **carbonated drinks**.

4 At what three stages does quality control take place?

....

....

....

5 Choose the correct words from the options given to complete the following sentences.

appearance　　**quality**　　**specification**　　**inspected**　　**final product**　　**fails**

During manufacture food is .... to ensure that the shape, size, ... ,

taste and texture meet the .... If it .... to meet these standards it

will affect the overall .... of the ....

6 Circle the correct options in the following sentences.

a) One-off production is used for making **identical products** / **prototypes in a test kitchen**.

b) Mass production **takes place in a factory** / **doesn't rely on specialised equipment**.

c) Batch production is **also known as jobbing** / **used by small scale manufacturers**.

d) Continuous flow **is used for making products twenty four seven** / **takes place in a test kitchen**.

7 Explain how ingredients are listed on labels.

8 What do the following symbols mean?

Symbol	
PET (1)	
alu	
RECYCLABLE STEEL	
(recycle)	
35	
(carton recycle)	
(tidy man)	

9 Which of the following statements are true? Tick the correct options.

A Computers are used for manufacturing because they don't make mistakes. ◯

B Computers are slower than people doing the same task. ◯

C Computers can detect things that the human eye can't see. ◯

D Computers are less hygienic than people. ◯

E Computers need highly-skilled technicians for programming and maintenance. ◯

Answers

QUICK TEST ANSWERS

Page 5

1. People under medical supervision, people with special dietary needs.
2. True
3. You can maintain a healthy weight by balancing the calories you eat with being physically active.
4. You should cut down on fat, sugar and salt.
5. True

Page 7

1. Manufacturers produce healthy option foods because many consumers are concerned about healthy eating.
2. Margarine is fortified with Vitamins A and D.
3. True
4. False
5. Your body needs energy for all bodily functions, such as breathing, pumping blood, digestion and brain activity.

Page 9

1. Protein is needed by the body for growth and repair.
2. If we eat too much protein it's used for energy or stored as fat.
3. True
4. True
5. Plant-based proteins are fortified with vitamins and minerals.

Page 11

1. Fat provides energy, keeps us warm, protects internal organs, and contains fat soluble vitamins A and D.
2. It's better to replace saturated fat with unsaturated fat to reduce cholesterol.
3. False
4. The correct word is monosaccharide.
5. Long distance runners eat starchy foods like pasta so that energy is released slowly through the race.

Page 13

1. Vitamins are composed of carbon, hydrogen and oxygen.
2. Vitamin C is found in citrus fruits.
3. False
4. Sodium
5. Iron
6. False

ANSWERS TO PRACTICE QUESTIONS

Page 14–15

1. A, F, G, H.
2. DRV stands for dietary reference values.
3. reducing, fat, sugar, salt, NSP (fat, sugar and salt can be **in any order**).
4. **a)** high blood pressure
   b) diabetes
   c) increasing
   d) coronary heart disease
   e) osteoarthritis
   f) some cancers.
5. High Biological Value proteins contain all the essential amino acids. Low Biological Value proteins lack one or more of the essential amino acids.
6. A, B, F.
7. **a)** bland
   b) easy
   c) 60 per cent.
8. **a)** soya beans
   b) mycoprotein
   c) wheat and vegetable protein
   d) soya beans.
9. B
10. B

QUICK TEST ANSWERS

Page 17

1. **Any three from**: raw or partially cooked egg, unpasteurised milk or milk products, liver and liver products, undercooked meat, cook-chill foods (unless heated thoroughly to 72°C), pâté, soil on fruit and vegetables, shark, swordfish, marlin.
2. Sword fish should be avoided during pregnancy because it contains mercury, and may harm development of the baby's nervous system.
3. **In any order**: high blood pressure, smoking, high cholesterol levels.
4. False
5. Lactase

Page 19

1. False
2. Gluten
4. beef, beef products.
5. True

Page 21

1. By checking that the packet has the vegetarian symbol, or checking the ingredients list.
2. without, lifestyle.
3. Fair trade products guarantee that farmers and workers get a fair price for their produce.

Page 23

1. Food miles means the distance food travels from where it's produced to where it's eaten.
2. False
3. Methane gas.
4. Carbon dioxide.
5. Beef and lamb.

Answers

Factors Affecting Consumer Choice (cont.)

ANSWERS TO PRACTICE QUESTIONS
Page 24–25
1. **a)** calcium
   b) moderation
   c) milk
   d) severe
   e) wheat
   f) beef.
2. Vegetarians may eat animal products like eggs, milk and cheese (made using vegetable rennet). Vegans don't eat any food from animals: this includes dairy products and honey.
3. A, B, D, E, F.

4. farmers, fair price, goods, environmentally, education, farming, tea, Africa.
5. A, E.
6. GM plant foods are being used to increase crop production. They can be modified to use less water, be disease and pest resistant, be a better colour, have a higher protein content, or withstand cold conditions.
7. one third, out of date, thrown away, landfill sites, methane, GHG.
8. Beef and lamb produce methane, which is twenty times more harmful than carbon dioxide.
9. The trees in the rain forests use up carbon dioxide. If they're cut down to grow palm for oil, the carbon dioxide will build up, contributing to global warming.

Cooking with Food

QUICK TEST ANSWERS
Page 27
1. True
2. Tomato, wine, yoghurt.
3. **In any order:** tuna, salmon and prawns, or any other suitable fish.
4. False
Page 29
1. Milk is heat treated to extend shelf life and kill bacteria.
2. 72°C
3. Dried milk.
4. **In any order:** butter, cream, cheese, yoghurt.
5. Yoghurt is made by adding a bacterial culture to milk.
Page 31
1. Cereals are edible seeds of cultivated grasses.
2. Starch
3. Fruit and vegetables are available all year round due to improved technology and production methods, and better transportation links.
4. Fruit and vegetables should be cooked in a small amount of water to reduce nutrient loss.
5. False
6. When eggs are heated they coagulate.
Page 33
1. Fat is a solid at room temperature, oil is liquid at room temperature.
2. True
3. Fat keeps a product moist for longer.
4. Sugar is produced from sugar cane and sugar beet.
5. Too much sugar leads to tooth decay.
6. True

ANSWERS TO PRACTICE QUESTIONS
Page 34–35
1. pressure blasting, sieve, removed, slurry, sausages, meat.
2. B, C, E, G.
3. **a)** salmon
   b) cod
   c) plaice
   d) prawns
   e) mussels.
4. Fish is a high risk food because it's a moist protein food, and prone to carrying bacteria.
5. Homogenised, milk, tiny holes, pressure, break, can't.
6. UHT milk – also known as 'long life' milk
   Sterilised milk – has its flavour altered
   Dried milk – the type of milk often used by manufacturers
   Evaporated milk – sealed in a can
   Pasteurised milk – heated to 72°C for 15 seconds and cooled rapidly to 10°C or below
   Semi-skimmed milk – has some of the cream removed.
7. **Any one from:** soya milk, rice milk, coconut milk, oat milk.
8. **a)** churning **b)** fat **c)** solid **d)** bacteria.
9. Garnish – savoury dishes
   Binding – beefburgers
   Glazing – pastry
   Emulsification – mayonnaise
   Coating – fish
   Aeration – swiss roll
   Coagulation – lemon curd

Functional Properties of Food

QUICK TEST ANSWERS
Page 37
1. False
2. A suspension forms when solids don't mix in a liquid.
3. Flour and milk form the gel in white sauce.
4. Pre-gelatinised starches thicken instantly.
5. Egg yolk acts as an emulsifier in mayonnaise to hold the oil and vinegar together.
6. False

Page 39
1. Glutenin, gliadin and water are needed to make gluten.
2. Soft margarine and lard are good choices for making pastry because they can be rubbed in easily.
3. False
4. Lime juice gives key lime pie its thick consistency.
5. True
6. Acetic acid gives a sharp flavour to salad dressings.

Answers

Functional Properties of Food (cont.)

Page 41
1. Raising agents can be added to a mixture mechanically or as an ingredient.
2. Air, steam and carbon dioxide make products light.
3. The conditions needed for yeast to grow are warmth, liquid, food and time.
4. Baking powder is a mixture of bicarbonate of soda, an acid, and a starchy filler.
5. True

Page 45
1. True
2. Convection takes place in air or liquid.
3. **In any order**: creaming, sieving, whisking.
4. **In any order**: bulk ingredient, forms structure, dextrinisation of starch gives colour.
5. Yeast
6. True

Page 47
1. **In any order**: sauces add flavour, moisture and nutritive value.

2. True
3. 60℃
4. False

ANSWERS TO PRACTICE QUESTIONS
Page 48–49
1. synerisis, pre-gelatinised, acidity.
2. gas, emulsifier, dissolved, suspension, solid.
3. A, C, E.
4. Raising agents work by incorporating a gas into a mixture. When the gas is heated it expands.
5. **a)–c) in any order:** air, steam, carbon dioxide.
6. **A** air, **B** CO_2, **C** steam, **D** CO_2, **E** CO_2.
7. A, C, D, F, G, H.
8. **In any order:** warmth, liquid, food, time.
9. a) self raising
   b) washing
   c) acid.
10. C

Making Food Safe

QUICK TEST ANSWERS
Page 50
1. Enzymes and micro-organisms must be controlled to extend the shelf life of food.
2. True
3. It causes the flesh of the fruit to turn brown – spoilage.
4. Add lemon juice.

Page 53
1. False
2. Probiotic bacteria are useful because they help digestion.
3. Fats and oils are low risk foods.
4. Clostridium Botulinum.
5. Staphylococcus Aureus.

Page 55
1. The danger zone.
2. True
3. 1–5℃
4. True
5. pH 3.5
6. MAP stands for Modified Atmospheric Packaging.

Page 57
1. A red chopping board should be used for raw meat.
2. A blue plaster with a metallic strip.
3. True
4. True
5. Irradiation.
6. Reducing temperature.

Page 59
1. False
2. 1–5℃
3. In 90 minutes or less.
4. An Environmental Health officer.
5. False
6. Accelerated freeze drying foods are restored by adding water.

Page 61
1. False
2. HTST means high temperature, short time.
3. Sterilisation
4. False
5. No

ANSWERS TO PRACTICE QUESTIONS
Page 62–63
1. C
2. A, D, E, F, G.
3. a) visible
   b) acid
   c) 70℃
   d) can
   e) can't.
4. single, rapidly, harmful, food poisoning, cheese, probiotic, digestion.
5. Without moisture bacteria can't grow. Moisture can be removed by dehydration, or turned into a solid by freezing. Salt and sugar concentrations reduce the moisture available.
6. A.
7. Cross contamination means transferring bacteria from one food to another.
8. B
9. B, D, E, F.
10. The E number shows that an additive has passed European Community Safety Standards.

Designing Food Products

QUICK TEST ANSWERS

Page 67
1. Lifecycle
2. The product specification is developed once the final dish has been designed.
3. True
4. Manufacturing specification.

Page 71
1. Portion control is used to ensure that all the products are identical.
2. Questionnaires provide primary research information.
3. True
4. Spreadsheet
5. True

Page 73
1. **In any order**: designers use small electrical equipment to obtain consistent results, guarantee the quality of the outcome, and avoid human error.
2. Money.
3. True
4. The HACCP procedure.
5. **In any order:** safety switches, guards, emergency stop buttons.

Page 75
1. False
2. Blind testing.
3. Hedonic rating is used to find out which product people like best.
4. Smiley faces.

Page 77
1. Discriminatory testing is used to see if people can tell the difference between two very similar samples.
2. Two
3. Another name for attribute testing is star profile / radar graph.
4. True
5. The terminator symbol shows the start or end of the system.
6. Decision symbol, i.e. a question with a 'yes' or 'no' answer.

ANSWERS TO PRACTICE QUESTIONS
Page 78–79
1. C, D, G.
2. Portion control, shape, written.
3. D
4. Primary research is collecting your own original information, which didn't exist before. Secondary research is using information already collected by someone else.
5. B, C, F, G, H.
6. It's done speedily and accurately, avoiding human error.
7. B
8. A, B, E.
9. A not A testing, attribute testing, triangle testing, paired preference testing, hedonic rating.
10.

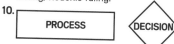

Food Manufacturing

QUICK TEST ANSWERS
Page 83
1. A prototype is made in a test kitchen.
2. CAM stands for Computer Aided Manufacture.
3. Quality assurance guarantees quality.
4. Quality control is a part of the quality assurance process.
5. False
6. A Trading Standards officer checks that labels are accurate.

Page 85
1. A hazard is anything that may go wrong and cause harm to someone.
2. HACCP stands for Hazard Analysis and Critical Control Points.
3. FIFO stands for First In First Out.
4. False
5. Remedial action is the last stage in a HACCP chart.

Page 87
1. A legal requirement means that it has to be included by law.
2. Yes
3. False
4. Volume
5. No

Page 89
1. True
2. Paperboard is waxed to make it water resistant.
3. Easy to open.
4. True
5. PS (expanded polystyrene) is brittle.

ANSWERS TO PRACTICE QUESTIONS
Page 90–91
1. A, D, E, G.
2. a) chemical
   b) contamination by bacteria, e.g. salmonella
   c) physical.
3. a) cheap b) breakable c) recyclable d) lightweight
   e) yoghurt containers f) carbonated drinks.
4. **In any order:** during design, during manufacture, at the end of manufacturing.
5. inspected, appearance, specification, fails, quality, final product.
6. a) prototypes in a test kitchen
   b) takes place in a factory
   c) used by small scale manufacturers
   d) is used for making products twenty four seven.
7. Ingredients are listed in descending order of weight on labels.
8. SPI System (PET numbers from 1–7 indicate type of plastic)

 Mobius loop – packaging is recyclable

 35 per cent of recycled materials used.

 Recyclable aluminium

Glass can be recycled and should be put in a bottle bank

 Recyclable steel

Do not litter

9. A, C, E.

Index

ACKNOWLEDGEMENTS

Thank you to Jessica Parkinson for proofreading the revision guide from a child's perspective.

The authors and publisher are grateful to the copyright holders for permission to use quoted materials and images.

p.4 eatwell plate (Food Standards Agency) © Crown copyright material is reproduced with the permission of the Controller of HMSO and Queen's Printer for Scotland; traffic light labelling: Food Standards Agency, www.eatwell.gov.uk; Guide Line Daily Amounts label: Food and Drink Federation, www.fdf.org.uk. **p.5** Food Standards Agency logo: Food Standards Agency, www.eatwell.gov.uk; iStockphoto.com / technotr. **p.8** 2008 Jupiterimages Corporation; iStockphoto.com / Helle Bro Clemmensen. **p.9** Tivall: Goodness Foods, www.goodnessdirect.co.uk; tofu pieces: Cauldron, Premier Foods. **p.10** iStockphoto.com / Suzannah Skelton; iStockphoto.com / Dori OConnell. **p.11** 2008 Jupiterimages Corporation. **p.16** iStockphoto.com / Chris Schmidt. **p.17** Alpro soya milk: Alpro UK Ltd, www.alprosoya.co.uk. **p.18** Petits pains: Livwell Ltd, www.livwell.eu; crossed grain symbol: Coeliac UK, www.coeliac.org.uk. **p.19** iStockphoto.com / Nancy Louie. **p.20** Vegetarian Society logo: The Vegetarian Society of the United Kingdom, Ltd, www.vegsoc.org, www.youngveggie.org; Vegan Society logo: The Vegan Society, www.vegansociety.com. **p.21** Red Tractor logo: Assured Food Standards, www.redtractor.org.uk; Fairtrade. **p.23** 2008 Jupiterimages Corporation. **p.27** iStockphoto.com / Linda Steward. **p.28** 2008 Jupiterimages Corporation. **p.29** iStockphoto.com / Ina Peters. **p.32** 2008 Jupiterimages Corporation. **p.36** 2008 Jupiterimages Corporation. **p.38** iStockphoto.com / Joern Rynio; iStockphoto.com / Seniz Yoruk. **p.40** iStockphoto.com / Martin McElligott. **p.42** iStockphoto.com / Nancy Louie. **p.44** iStockphoto.com / Heath Doman. **p.45** 2008 Jupiterimages Corporation. **p.46** iStockphoto.com / Chris Elwell. **p.47** 2008 Jupiterimages Corporation; iStockphoto.com / Dave White; tofu pieces: Cauldron, Premier Foods. **p.52** iStockphoto.com; 2008 Jupiterimages Corporation. **p.57** iStockphoto.com / Terry Reimink. **p.58** 2008 J Sainsbury Plc. **p.59** iStockphoto.com / Sean Locke. **p.60** iStockphoto.com / Mark Yuill. **p.64** Free range eggs: Chippindale Foods Limited, www.chippindalefoods.co.uk; shortbread and quince jelly: Sussex and the City, www.sussexandthecity.co.uk. **p.65** University of Abertay Dundee, www.foodinnovation.abertay.ac.uk; 2008 Jupiterimages Corporation. **p.66** iStockphoto.com / Julien Grondin. **p.68** iStockphoto.com / LaHeather Massengale. **p.69** Jam tarts: Livwell Ltd, www.livwell.eu; iStockphoto.com / Martin Garnham. **p.71** 2007 Jupiterimages Corporation. **p.72** Bridge © The *Focus on Food* Campaign www.focusonfood.org Photography by Richard Moran. **p.73** iStockphoto.com / Clayton Hansen. **p.74** Sensory science photograph: The University of Nottingham, School of Biosciences (Division of Food Sciences), www.nottingham.ac.uk/biosciences. **p.80** iStockphoto.com / Dr. Heinz Linke. **p.82** iStockphoto.com / Talshiar.